The Painful Truth

a path toward peace

wrestling with the core technique of the Buddha's enlightenment

GARY ALLAN RATSON, MD

Tellwell Talent
www.tellwell.ca

ISBN
978-0-2288-3907-1 (Hardcover)
978-0-2288-3906-4 (Paperback)
978-0-2288-3908-8 (eBook)

DEDICATION

To Dad,

Nate Ratson.

Here's to carrying on the family tradition

— peace and quiet.

TABLE OF CONTENTS

ACKNOWLEDGMENTS

Endless gratitude to Kate "Kathy" Erickson,
the perfect person in the perfect place and time
to introduce me to Vipassana Meditation.
I.O.U.

A true Bodhisattva, the late S.N. Goenka succeeded
in bringing pure Dhamma to the world.
Continuity of practice is the only way
to honor his memory.

Selfless Dhamma volunteers
embody the teaching daily
with compassion and sympathetic joy
as the lifeblood of the centers worldwide.
With Metta.

AUTHOR'S NOTE

This original daily journal follows seventeen years of learning and adapting to the Vipassana lifestyle. The **bold** fonts depict the Vipassana instructions as they are heard during meditation sessions or recalled at other times. *Italicized* passages represent the insights and experiences during formal meditation sittings and various moments of contemplation.

1

FREE FALLING

The pain was totally worth it. Twenty years of scouring health research gave no warnings of falling ass-backwards into the happiest day of my life. Ten years of searching for meaning unknowingly set the table for the most significant day ever. One year after sailing the world in the twisted hope of a near-death experience, I was graced with a near-life encounter without going anywhere. Only after accepting my dead-end pursuit did a life-giving door open up during ten days of Vipassana meditation.

I declared my good fortune the greatest human experience. Hours of physical torture allowed a glimpse into the subtle underbelly of both suffering and wellbeing. An agonizing life review clarified the meaning of all my life choices, obstacles, and mistakes. Infinite gratitude was matched only by a new-order humility. I got the keys to the rest of my life that up until then had been parked and abandoned. That was some happiest day.

Halfway through medical school I knew I had set myself up for disaster. Even before being accepted I was reading *The Confessions of a Medical Heretic*. I told my entrance examiners about my interest in fitness and nutrition but none of them twigged onto directing me to naturopathy. How did I get past the front gates?

The hospital wards were not welcoming to my vague notions of health and wellbeing. Naïve resistance to the medical way of being created the same stress in me as I saw in the patients. Both their faces and my guts screamed for something more profound than pills, surgery and an expedited b'bye. The sterile environment zapped any opportunity for genuine healing, lasting change, or God forbid, the meaning of illness. Graduation would prove to be the most miserable day of my life.

I became increasingly aloof and alone. Relationships with classmates were slipping away with my confidence, enthusiasm, and career plans. I was really just auditing the course. Circumstances played right into my hands as every rotation in every department had the quietest month on record. No emergencies, no codes, and few night calls allowed me to sleep through my internship— literally and figuratively. The grunt work on wards is miserable enough even when drinking the Kool-Aid. My home brew was a sad mixture of disappointment, guilt and shame. With a little emotional intelligence, I might have made the best of a bad situation.

A torn knee ligament at our third-year Halloween bash (don't ask) and a weak final exam gave me cover to take a year off. The dean had me into his office to confirm what was left of my sanity. The next year, faculty policy was changed to limit student sabbaticals to medical research or related activity. Just one of many infamous firsts or lasts in my college career. Anyway, first stop: Hawaii. *Aloha!*

Then as a poor man's psychiatrist, I tended bar for most of that year. That job was uneventful if you don't count the drinking, the parties, and the plastic surgery to repair tendons and nerves in my left hand. I ripped the neck off a two-litre bottle of laughin' Lenz Moser along with the cork one night at work. With the summer to recover I had a newfound appreciation of medical school.

Unexpectedly, a charismatic orthopedic surgeon gave an inspiring talk in the fall that woke me up to sports medicine. A two-month elective at his Halifax clinic motivated me to finish my degree. I was invited back after internship to work at this progressive multi-discipline clinic with a nutritionist and physiotherapy. The attached racquetball courts, gym, and spa were an embarrassment of riches before having accomplished anything. I could not have found a more supportive place to flourish. There was no reason for continued defiance of conventional medicine, but I found some.

Cynicism grew from college athletes seeking performance-enhancing drugs. Resentment came from disability insurance prolonging a victim mentality in patients. Skepticism peaked with systemic conflicts of interest with drug companies and medical research. These were easy targets of my own ignorance and self-doubt. High expectations for the perfect job were not enough to explain this level of career anxiety and despair.

In the summer before medical school I had the choice between staying in Winnipeg for medicine or joining three buddies at a Toronto chiropractic college. I went with the easier, cheaper, more prestigious option, assuming more career opportunities. Years later, my friends assured me that my contrary attitudes would have followed me no matter which path I took. The evidence for that was not limited to my professional life.

My excuses for leaving a marriage within a year would change every year for ten years. It *was* complicated. Respite from fighting the world and the sudden acceptance into society made it feel like a good idea at the time. The public shame and humiliation were worse than my private career hell. A psychiatrist from Physician Helpline turfed me to a new-age bookstore when I refused to see any connection between personal and professional dysfunction. It was all self-help from there.

Like a kid in a candy store, I devoured titles from every bookshelf. The first one that caught my eye was *A Brief History of Everything* by Ken Wilber. A self-taught philosopher, he spent years rearranging hundreds of books on the living room floor until an integrative vision of all disciplines emerged. This ingenious way of seeing all things in their proper place resonated with my poorly articulated disconnect with civilized society.

Reading Wilber's earlier work and each new hardcover as it came out in the 90s substituted for much-needed therapy. Accepting the partial truths of all disciplines gave science, psychology, and mystic traditions equal respect. Importantly, his integral theory acknowledged the reality of individual and collective consciousness, which hinted at why medicine got under my skin.

Every discipline could now be seen through this unifying perspective. The possibility of accepting the good things in Western medicine also allowed the reasonable parts of Eastern healing, energy psychology, and new-age physics to ring true.

Holistic ideas were confirming what I naturally assumed— brain peptides were found throughout the immune, endocrine, and peripheral nervous systems; cells of all organs respond to what is going on in the mind; love and purpose correlated with longevity more than fitness and diet; quality of life was more about resilience and personal freedom than nutritional supplements or lifestyle. The growing list of psychosomatic illnesses cemented the notion that limiting beliefs, mistaken identity, and subconscious stress all contribute to disease. I had found sympatico with a faraway tribe of independent thinkers unavailable in the classroom. Still, it didn't do much for my career.

Ancient traditions have complex healing systems way beyond the scope of modern understanding. How did diverse early cultures create comparative bodies of knowledge isolated by time and distance? The contemplative component stood out to me more than mere trial and error. Still, I had a hard time believing that today's alternative practitioners were tapping into the same intuitive awareness.

Complementary medicine was used for symptomatic relief just as allopathic treatment. I was suspicious of modern docs using ancient therapies to their full effect outside the original context. I was skeptical that contemporary healers could rebalance blockages in the chakras or meridians. I was not even certain that spiritual energy or subtle anatomy was real or accessible. And yet partial truths persisted. Consciousness remained a key takeaway from all sources of healing wisdom.

A subtler approach to health would balance and allow rather than block or stimulate the biology with drugs. It would take an uncommon knowledge to utilize the limiting truths of all disciplines so as to not make things worse.

Generally, we wait for the next generation of telescopes and microscopes before seeing the next iteration of reality. The visible rainbow is only a tiny portion of the electromagnetic spectrum. Most of the matter and energy in the universe is considered missing or dark. Maybe that is why most of our consciousness remains subconscious. Our limited awareness would explain not seeing that deeply into things. Still, I could not cut myself slack for being in the dark about formal education rubbing me the wrong way.

I saw that hidden beliefs and blind habits were making most of our lifestyle choices. Unexamined attitudes and values were driving relationships and careers. Inner development shaped the self-sense and worldview that determined stress or success. I was leaning toward the idea that health and happiness merely reflect our level of awareness.

Salvaging this life of turmoil demanded using intuition with reason, creativity with logic. The picture of health I painted saw science unopposed to spirituality, transpersonal psychology compatible with quantum physics, and medicine aligned with consciousness. The highest wellbeing appeared sourced in the deeper meaning of purpose, love, responsibility, and freedom. Yet I had no conceivable way of increasing those qualities in myself.

Signs of heading in the right direction came from the recurring themes in reading and writing. Sharing my findings one day with like-minded souls might be rewarding. Good enough just proving to friends and family that I had not gone over the deep end.

I left the sport medicine clinic out of similar unease that followed me through internship. A temporary job as a refracting eye physician allowed me to survive with the fewest drugs for me and my patients. That one-year plan turned into ten years while looking for something better. Reading saved my soul—if only on life support. It was no way to live, but I saw no way out.

With a decade of notes piling up, the inspiration to express the ideas as poems came as a fun way to avoid proper grammar. The courage to paint the full picture in a book came simply from needing something to show for my efforts. Maybe the confidence helped me to take the next step. It had to be destiny to leave everything behind because there was nothing to leave. I sold the house and quit my job in a desperate attempt to tempt fate. I concluded from years of research that change doesn't happen unless life-changing events change it for you.

I was more of a nester than gatherer. But eager to act different to be different, I inquired into an ad for a 'round the world sailing adventure in a medical travel journal—no experience necessary. I had no great desire to see the world but the possibility of a near-death experience, or perhaps saving a life, would give my head the shake it needed. I took all my notes, but the undulant sea and exciting ports of call delayed writing until disembarking in Bali, Indonesia.

Sailing is defined as travelling from port to port in need of repairs—not to mention drinking and debauchery. I was all-in from Florida to Australia, but the Pacific was too passive for life-threatening encounters. The six weeks motoring without wind or land between the Galapagos and French Polynesia was like twelve guys being quarantined with flu.

Yes, we slammed a few yachts in a Trinidad marina, dragged a coral reef in Fiji, almost jumped ship in a Niue tropical storm, and hit a cruise ship line in Tahiti—nothing to write home about. Even the sharks, whales, and manta rays were user friendly. A few docs living their retirement dream did not look kindly on me just wanting to get out of the house. My wish for a ritual drowning and rebirth did not materialize. In that sense, nothing much happened.

The happiest time of my landlubber life was the two months writing in Bali. The island that survived on tourism was almost deserted after 9/11. Anonymity on an island of two million people meant not having to constantly explain myself or feel the judgement of others. Those tension-free weeks exposed all the energy I had wasted pacifying others.

The sixty-day time limit on the Balinese visa forced me to finish a first draft of *The Meaning of Health*. After a year without giving it much thought I wrote it all out by hand during a month by the pool. So, something good did happen. In month two, typing up the scribble at an internet café was a full daily grind. Best job ever.

Research confirmed that purpose, love, responsibility, and freedom were synonymous with wellbeing. There was good reason for medicine to ignore this as there was precious little they could do about it. The essentials of health required a deliberate life path. Turns out, healing was indeed a spiritual journey as identity, beliefs, and values all had to be confronted and challenged.

Arduous as it is, genetic expression and immune defenses depend on an evolving character. A continuum of consciousness underlies the range of illness severity, treatment response, and the degree of suffering. The security of increasing awareness had more appeal to me than chasing the next life-saving drug, cholesterol guideline, or food pyramid. We all want to be healthy and happy, but ironically, it is our level of consciousness that determines what that means and how we go about it. The meaning of health meant discovering the meaning of consciousness. This could take a while.

I was happy to piece together a vision of health I could live with. It all pointed to the recurring truth that was sabotaging my career. Everything happens in consciousness before being expressed in the body. Waging war on cancer, addiction, and depression ignored the inner fight that was there all along. Healing looked more like surrendering and forgiving than doubling down on resisting and suppressing. I could have taken my own advice instead of fighting a culture that uses a pill for every ill.

Writing is mostly rewriting, so I spent the next year massaging the manuscript with a fresh start in the fresh air of beautiful British Columbia. Finding good intel was like pulling teeth, but I finally had a satisfying view of the world. I wrote the book I had needed to read all this time. If this was as good as it gets, I was fine with it.

The search was over. A bittersweet moment was admitting the work was merely an intellectual endeavor. In no way had I transitioned into the loving being I could only imagine. I did not embody the highest character I admired in others. I did not achieve my dreamed-of life purpose. Book smarts do not move the needle any more than sailing the seven seas. But scratching a lifelong itch felt darn good, even with no plans to do anything with it. *C'est la vie.*

A funny thing happens when you stop struggling and accept your circumstances. Kathy was a new friend who had reviewed my book. She had just returned from a grueling ten-day meditation retreat that she knew I would love. I knew that reading about meditation was even less effective than reading about health. Any lofty spiritual attainments meant years of sitting in India at the foot of a guru. That wasn't going to happen.

I was impressed with the first thing I saw on the <u>www. dhamma.org</u> website. Meditation centers in this little-known unnamed tradition were spreading around the world with no paid teachers or staff. As a charitable organization, it was run only by volunteers that had completed a course themselves. There was no charge for the teaching or room and board as per the Buddha's designs to humble the ego. This was all a powerful endorsement of something special.

The centers were built and sustained by donations only from those having sat a full course. It sounded too good to be true but good enough to get on the wait list for the next course. I had long given up on life-changing adventures. With no expectations, it would be a nice getaway in the country to enjoy vegetarian food and lose a few pounds on the cheap.

2

THE PAINFUL TRUTH

The story of truth has been told repeatedly
throughout the ages but it bears telling again.

—David Hawkins MD
The Eye of the I

March 12ᵗʰ, 2003
1:30 p.m.

The anthem that had colored my adventure out of Winnipeg two years before came roaring back. "Free Falling" by Tom Petty played in my head as I hoisted my backpack. This leap of faith was not as scary as walking away from work. Ten days without talking did not alarm me. Ten days of breakfast and lunch with no dinner was fine. Ten days of sitting on the floor could be a problem. My main concern was ten days!

The wait list had opened within days, leaving a few more to contemplate the prospects of a long-drawn-out silence. Removing my watch was all I could think of in the hopes of encouraging a timeless experience. Outside my building, a suspended moment in time caught me before hopping into my ride to the meditation center. I froze for a second over the mailbox with the manuscript of *The Meaning of Health*, realizing that chapter of my life had been literally sealed. Bringing me back was the eerie soundtrack from *Déjà Vu* with Denzel Washington, which I had just seen. "Time Is On My Side" by the Stones replaced the last earworm for the foreseeable future.

We arrived early afternoon at the one-year old bungalow carved into the forest above farmland, two hours east of Vancouver between Hope and Merritt, BC. With signage directing parking and registration there were no obvious signs of anyone running the place. A central courtyard was surrounded by twenty-five semi-private rooms with four-inch foam mattresses and a communal bathroom. No problem. Sailing makes you pretty low-maintenance. The clearly posted instructions suggested a well-run operation and created unexpected anticipation.

I had given away most of my books as a letting-go exercise. Hopefully, writing everything else down had opened up some room in my head for something new to get in. I had held onto the pipedream that real health could not be bought or sold, health care would be free of commercial bias. Yet here it was.

Complete silence and segregation would help with distractions. All other rules were for the support of the students rather than servers' convenience. I breezed through the moral precepts—no killing, stealing, lying, intoxicants or sexual misconduct—without giving them much thought. No exercise sounded stifling. The 4:30 a.m. - 9:00 p.m. timetable looked daunting until I calculated seven hours of sleep. *Time is on my side . . . .*

I had read about cults; this wasn't that. There was no obligation, joining, or converting. There was no charismatic leader taking over personal lives. I did not see a teacher or anyone really in charge of the few hippies fussing about in the kitchen. There was nothing to suggest a new-age religion or a spiritual ashram. The modern building had no images, statues, or icons, only a few homely plants against bare walls.

Despite enjoying books on Buddhist psychology, I never considered the actual reality of enlightenment or if the Buddha was a real person. I had just read a free booklet on the Buddha's four noble truths from a vegan Chinese restaurant. This is suffering, this is the cause of suffering, this is the cure of suffering, and this is the path of liberation from suffering. It was obvious yet meaningless without knowing what was meant by "this!"

There were no red flags or concerns with the introductory talk. An interesting mix of ages, genders, and races was comforting and reassuring. After hearing a long list of regulations, we were repeatedly asked to reconsider if we were up to the task. No one left. A light meal followed before entering the mediation hall at 8:00 p.m. for the opening instructions of the technique.

I took my spot along the back wall as requested. My back should be fine at the right angle created by a foam brick leaning on a yoga block. Unexpectedly, a male and female assistant merely controlled the audio and video of the original teacher. Unusual throaty chanting opened the course before the ritual acceptance of the teaching and vow of silence that suddenly created a serious atmosphere.

S.N. Goenka was worldly and well-spoken, reassuring with preliminary comments. Vipassana means to see things as they really are, not as you may want them to be: Insight Meditation. My interest was piqued with the somber words of why we were here – *to realize the truth of mind and body as taught by Gautama the Buddha. You are here to subdue the monkey mind and liberate yourself of all suffering.* This sounded like the real deal. No timeline given.

Leaning against the wall in my jeans, the instructions to feel the touch of the breath as it passes through the nostrils are not as easy as they sound. A slightly forced breath is permitted to localize the sensation before returning to the natural flow. Within minutes I doubt that it is even possible to observe the breath without affecting it.

The best I can do is a slightly forced inhale, followed by an outgoing sigh. The immediate goal of one-minute uninterrupted attention on the breath will take some time. My next difficulty is dropping the silent mantra I had used intermittently for twenty years for stress relief and creativity. Endless thoughts are an expected distraction. Repeatedly returning to the breath without judgement gets really old really fast. The one-hour opening session is done before quietly avoiding eye contact back to the dorm.

Day One

Four a.m. comes quickly for two hours of breath work before breakfast. Blanketed in a chair in my room, the heated concrete floors are comfy on the feet. The dark early morning is less distracting until sleep tugs at the brain. I plan to redouble my efforts today to prove myself wrong about influencing the breath for as long as it takes. I have ten days.

Day Two

It is halfway through day two before the breath takes priority over my habitual mantra. My back feels ok against the wall for a one-hour session at a time. Slightly forced breathing helps hold the focus, but a solid minute is an eternity. In the effort, I miss many of the periodic instructions. The evening discourse mentions something about other sensations that may appear in the area above the upper lip. **Simply note anything that arises without reacting, then return to the breath.**

I fashioned a routine of 4:00 a.m. showering and 5:00 p.m. teeth-brushing that allowed me to drop into bed by 9:01 p.m. As opposed to early a.m., which is most conducive for concentration, the 11th hour brings crushing fatigue.

Day Three

By the morning of day three I am getting into the groove as a mundane itch arises on my upper lip. Before I mindlessly scratch it away, the wherewithal comes to observe the dust-mote-shaped tickle. Awareness of this now pinching target is easier than the light touch of the breath, sustaining itself longer than expected. It is something else to do. Within a minute the tiny irritant gains the strength of a pulling thread. The squiggly obsession starts burrowing itself deep into the skin. Looking away eases the pressure while baring on it down doubles the size and force of the wriggling little prick. The rogue sensation easily holds my undivided attention. **Do not react mentally or physically to any sensation.** *The surrounding lip muscle begins twitching with mere observation. I follow the vibrating electrical charge as it shimmies through the lip and into the underlying bone. Retreating to the comfort zone of the breath, I compose myself and regroup.* **Do not give any meaning or importance to the arising sensations.** *I guess.*

The quivering pinpoint sluggishly leaves the designated area carving its way through the cheekbone like a dental procedure gone wrong. Each breath now provides the push along what seems a predetermined path. It reminds me of getting my teeth cleaned where distracting thoughts cannot break through the intense pressure. **Do not label the sensation, do not look for or avoid any particular sensation.**

Multiple laser-like beams similarly appear over the rest of the morning, cutting into facial bones and sinuses with surgical precision.

Further instructions are drowned out by the cracking and popping of bony joints and tight skull sutures. Yielding to the minimal guidance, I rest often at the edge of the nostrils while the spot-welders shiver in place. Nothing like this is in the brochure.

We cannot create sensation or determine when they pass away. *Concentration simply allows us to be aware of the reality that is already there. I get that. Meanwhile, the simple act of observing triggers the laser pointers to grind up the rest of my face with a good ten pounds of pressure. I am too occupied and fascinated to consider how or what is actually happening.*

The next step in the process is to increase the power of concentration by narrowing the focus on the breath to a yet smaller area above the lip. Ok. That does not seem necessary. I smile a crooked smile as Goenka mentions that this is the beginning of a surgical operation of the mind. Oh? My lip is swollen, my right eye is tearing and there is no suction available for the drool.

Seeking the truth here means no thinking, visualizing, or imagination allowed. Yet memories of acupuncture and Eastern therapies rattle around as an energy field envelopes my head and neck. The cervical spine is snapping and crackling in ways my chiropractor would die for. Fascination and curiosity keep fear and anxiety at bay. Watching sensations cannot possibly be harmful. Right? I have to trust the teaching, however vague and nonspecific it is.

Finally, I greeted lunch with one eye shut, nose dripping, and a half-frozen face. A private noon interview with the assistant teacher sounded reasonable. That was until a mid-morning check-in when I happened to mention alien light beams carving up my skull. His doubt and admonishment for the creative imagination stunned my expectations for unconditional acceptance, making me question the value of asking for help. I was going rogue.

Vipassana Day Four

I looked forward to the new daily postings for definitions, explanations, and timetabling. Day-four signage declared today was Vipassana Day. I thought we were doing Vipassana? Preoccupied by the faux root canal, I was slow to twig onto the incremental daily steps of the course.

I was all in. How often does something this dramatic happen with any therapy or technique anywhere? I knew that an elusive door to the essence of something had cracked open. It was a point of no return in terms of confronting head on whatever lay ahead. Sailing the Pacific had rocked me to sleep rather than rocking my worldview. Now just sitting there going nowhere, the depths of the mind promised to wake me up. And we hadn't even begun Vipassana.

It felt great be free of resistance for a change. I was familiar with the bits of ancient philosophy and modern physics allowing me to throw myself into the work. Everything I heard validated a decade of study, with the opportunity to take it beyond the books. Every therapy I ever heard of tried to make the subconscious mind conscious. Eastern healing was all about releasing and balancing blockages of subtle energy. Here, sensations that were previously unconscious were made conscious with nothing but attention and focus. These common origins of mind and body might blow my mind if they don't blow my head off first.

Things are getting real. The sacredness of the moment has me eagerly accepting the ritual chanting that sets the tone for learning Vipassana. The solemn environment inspires a real commitment to the ceremonial request to be taught the technique that the Buddha used to become enlightened. Then something about not moving at all during the group meditations raised a brow. Wait, what?

Vipassana begins with a strange croaking chant at a frequency I assume resonates with meditating minds. Attention still on the nostril/lip area, the energy cloud about my head paralyzes the thought process, leaving a striking wakefulness. I happily surrender any interest in the multiple pressure points settling deep into my face. Ten minutes in, Goenka surprises me by instructing us to transfer our focus to the very top of the head. Oh My God, I know what this is.

It takes some mental maneuvering to extricate my attention from a hypnotic attachment to the lip. With no actual thought, I recall a vague energetic importance of the crown of the head. Extended chanting keeps us engaged at the new point of contact. The command to observe any activity on the central seams of the skull confirms that the entire body may be consumed with the same electrical frenzy as the face.

Impersonal, essenceless sensations randomly arise and pass away without meaning. Calmly, objectively, dispassionately, observe whatever arises.

Soon enough, sweaty tingling breaks out over the area that was soft in the newborn. A new mental muscle is needed to move attention over the entire head in bite-size chunks watching for anything to emerge. The supportive guidance and all-consuming effort keep thoughts at bay. Not unexpectedly, the time to inch down the body means nesting is over. It is an excruciating wait for minute fluctuations before moving to the next part of the grid.

Without the flow of the breath, each fleeting sensation takes even more effort to feel. The one-minute time limit leaves most of my torso completely blank of activity. The painstaking work means cutting corners by counting the fingers and toes as one. And the groin. The level of difficulty just got supersized. The lip remains a welcome rest area to contemplate the four long days it took just to begin dissecting the mind.

The idea arises to feel all parts of the body simultaneously. This will take forever. Then a childhood memory of a guy on TV running back and forth to keep plates spinning on poles makes me smile. Even better, passing attention up and down the body like a hula hoop is worth a try. The Tasmanian Devil whipping up a tornado of awareness should do the job best, if not too exhausting. The mind does cartoons, right?

I knew the word equanimity as mental composure—even-handedness or level-headedness. I had never heard of the adjective form. The central command in Vipassana is to be equanimous—objective and detached toward all arising sensation. No matter how painful, irritating, or dramatic, do not react with any emotion, resistance, or desire. I did not think to include my desperation and impatience for results.

Day Five

I am now hip to the additional directives each day. Day five has us moving up from the toes to the head in a systematic doubling back over every part. Large blank areas are boring while angles and creases are painstaking. Equanimity is not possible any time soon and stretching the rules is inevitable. Hopefully I appear motionless as my eyes jump and roll to direct my attention to various parts. Extreme mental gymnastics are unavoidable in the face of mounting pain and pressure. The Tasmanian thing is overkill. It is obvious that full equanimity comes only with full liberation.

After one up-and-down cycle, pass your attention over the whole body en mass. *Hula hoop style? Scanning the whole body is like a paint roller covering the spots missed with the hand brush. My cheating heart tries to make use of the mind, now entrained with the breath. Just as yoga teachers curiously say "breathe into the stretch," each exhale now projects a literal breeze over a targeted patch of skin. Despite large blind areas on my torso, self-sustaining vibrations appear over most of the body like a living and breathing thing. Fascinating.*

Sparks and shocks are ignited in the wake of each passing round. Otherworldly sensations are confusing as I recall only a handful of sensory nerve receptors to account for pain, pressure, vibration, temperature, and proprioception. Then again, just seven colors of the rainbow generate an infinite palate. Signals from individual nerves coalesce into wafting sensations in the same way that neon bulbs on the Las Vegas strip only appear to be moving. The electricity is moving. Here, awareness is the conductor sweeping over the skin, informing the symphony of nerves what to play and how loud to play it.

Day Six

A golf-ball-sized bubble suddenly forms in my left flank mid-morning of day six. The discreet sphere between layers of back muscles is as real as anything. Working above, I leave the orb to fester until I come around to it. There are subtle vibrations throughout the body now most intense at the hips and knees. Strong pressure points persist in the face. The painless ball intensifies its presence without direct attention. Throughout the afternoon, the pulsating globe tunnels toward the lower point of the shoulder blade before disappearing. Thoughts of extra-terrestrial probing come to mind.

Another surprise came at the break when I effortlessly bent over the sink to throw water in my face. For a decade, low back pain had prohibited that motion. With normal x-rays and reasonable core strength, I assumed this is where I carried my stress. Back in the meditation hall, I confidently pulled my yoga brick away from the wall.

Creativity is not the same reacting to sensations—so says me. My next brilliant idea comes from that animated golf ball under the skin. Reality must include sensations inside the body. It couldn't hurt to sneak a peek.

Day Seven

After going unconscious overnight, it takes the full two-hour meditation early on day seven to really light up the body. Following a few faltering breaths up and down the body, I take the plunge directly into a thigh muscle that ignites a roaring electrical fire. The severity of the pain and regret is equaled by the fascination of the discovery.

Instructions allow for a detailed dissection of all gross sensations without giving any specifics. The mind reveals itself as a fine precision probe, cutting into different tissues with distinctive densities. Muscle, bone, and cartilage each feel unique in texture and strength. The lungs feel as spongy as in real life. The quality of sinuses, bone marrow, and joints remind me of eating chicken. The knife of awareness delicately slices into the eyeball's lens, iris, and retina. Gouging the liver and spleen makes me queasy and nauseous, forcing me to back off. How is this happening?

This bizarre experience is somehow familiar, yet I cautiously yield back to the breath and the skin. The effects of peering into the body feels more like doing than looking. It will take years to figure out this psychic surgery. Magnetic fields paralyze the mind, requiring some forcing of the breath just to move about.

Day Eight

By day eight, pulsations in the ears draw my attention to the heart. Working smart rather than hard, I figure that awareness might similarly entrain itself on the blood as it did with the breath. The rules did not caution against looking into the aorta. Tentatively breaching the thick muscular wall above the heart, my awareness is swiftly swept away with the current to the furthest reaches of the body. With each heartbeat pounding my knees, the thighs scream like red-hot pokers. Too much? I retreat to the breath but there is no going back.

I will never make it to the end of the hour. Schemes for rapid results turn into schemes for survival. Femurs are creaking and threatening to snap. Spinal joints are self-adjusting under duress. There is no escape as slight movements to ease the pressure simply inflame the situation. The generic instructions make for a lot of improvising.

The evening discourse cautions about piercing the skin until after a free flow over the entire surface is attained. Oops!

As a kid, I trusted dentists and doctors no matter the pain or discomfort. As a student, I had faith in my teachers no matter my struggle for understanding. Here, I was willing to endure whatever it took to know this otherwise inaccessible reality. But Goenka's unrelenting emphasis on equanimity had me second guessing my basic nature of facing the truth. It was alarming to think students were wasting time playing games with sensations at the expense of this opportunity of a lifetime. I could only hope that my curiosity and enthusiasm did not slow me down in the same way as desiring pleasure or avoiding the pain.

Day Nine

In the dark quiet morning of day nine, the possibility of the nervous system as an antenna in a conscious energy field became real. The concept of memories being stored like a chemical library in the brain never held water. It just may become self-evident that consciousness is the software that tells the brain how to think and what to do.

Inching my way to the opening at the base of the skull, I am struck by a sharp metal taste in my mouth. The glint of stainless steel near my brainstem stops me in my tracks. Before triggering a coma or quadriplegia, I retreat to the lip.

Sensations are most powerful where large nerves are exposed as above the collar bone, under the armpit, and the sciatic branches under the glutes. The thin bone of the crown allows the brain to resonate with the strongest vibrations. It is now making sense that the nervous system translates the subconscious bandwidths into the innumerable conscious sensations.

The need to peek into the brain comes with some trepidation. Carefully poking a magnetic finger through the paper-thin bone via the nose is met with an anticlimactic nothingness. The skull cavity is completely vacuous. No comment. I recall patients kept awake during brain surgery because of no pain perception. This lighthearted pause gives the confidence to breathe up and down the spinal cord that jabs and jolts like a twelve-string guitar.

More stunning is the unravelling of taut upper back strap muscles, times twenty-five years. These strands of paraspinals unwind like garden hoses gone wild. Jagged rocks then impale the shoulder blades. The legs roar with jet fuel, making the notion of arising and passing seem quaint. I imagined pulsed magnetic therapy combined with electro-acupuncture, with trigger point massage under thirty feet of water pressure, could account for ten percent of this pummeling.

Many old injuries are reawakened. This sharpened mind is cleaning up longstanding habits—that has got to improve form and function. The spine is held more erect than I can maintain on my own. My electromagnetic pointer continues to tease through delicate vessels and tissues. Awareness incidentally passes through the bladder like a live wire bubbling through water that later burns hot like a fever. With the compression of sitting, a nerve between my third and fourth toes splatters like bacon. The difference between Vipassana pain and everyday symptoms is more than confounding.

Nine o'clock could not come fast enough. Mercifully, sleep came by 9:02 p.m. Recognizing the origin of sixties artwork, I assumed these psychedelic dreams are safer than hallucinogenic ones. Four a.m. was easier with the zeal to see what happens next. Pangs of hunger dominated morning meditation with daydreams of breakfast. Somewhere in the background was the suggestion to pass through the spinal cord only after getting a free flow through the body. Ugh!!

And whatever you do, stay out of the organs. Ewe!

My current struggle echoed Goenka's own history with intractable migraines. His teacher refused him as a student unless he gave up the mundane goal of curing chronic pain. Like driving with the brakes on, craving relief is the very suffering that Vipassana targets. Physical healing must be left as a side effect of releasing subconscious stress. But relieving a decade of back pain would be hard to ignore.

Nothing on this journey would be clear until well down the road. The Buddha's middle path gave me cover for the middle ground of ignoring health only during meditation itself. If pure equanimity was the gatekeeper to the healing, then my wellness bias would be the conflicting issue. Yet the ultimate goal of complete liberation held little meaning being lifetimes away.

As with the morality piece, two steps forward and one step back would suffice to get the ball rolling. I trusted that my heart was in the right place since it got me to this point. My residual ignorance made endless mistakes inevitable but forgivable, notwithstanding the mental scribbling of my next exposé of medicine, psychology, and religion. Oops!

I knew what this meant. Vipassana offered the certainty and security unavailable anywhere in society. Beyond opinion and perception, consciousness had been objectively scrutinized by the Buddha. Lasting wisdom was not found in hard science but in subjectivity itself. Interpreting facts wisely required this greater context and meaning. This Wisdom Meditation reconciled the long-lost truth of spiritual clichés, inspired quotations, and philosophical ideals.

This was my Mt. Everest. No pain was too much, no sacrifice too great. Ten days of purging allowed an otherworldly peace and joy to shine through. Ten idle days oddly became an invigorating way to lose ten pounds. I could wait for the details and the molten lava to cool; renewed purpose in love, freedom, and responsibility will power the way. This inner adventure had permanently replaced the intellectual search.

The last official hour of the course was a guided loving-kindness meditation, meant as a salve for our open wounds. In spite of immense gratitude for this very moment, I did not see how the sentiment would ease ten days of exhaustion. An overflow of good-will absolutely resonated with all beings being free of all suffering. Still, in the wake of such a dramatic technique I was at a loss to feel the effectiveness of wishing and praying.

> *May I be free of anger, hatred, ill will, and animosity.*
> *May I generate only love, compassion,*
> *good will, and sympathetic joy.*
> *I forgive those who hurt me, intentionally or unintentionally.*
> *May those forgive me who I hurt,*
> *intentionally or unintentionally.*

Forgiving everyone everything really opened up the floodgates. For a good part of an hour after final Metta, giant tears pumped with each heartbeat, soaking my shirt. Resting in a peaceful field, I had no inclination to join the group that left to celebrate noble chattering in the dining hall. Ten more minutes to allow for stiff achy legs, I crawled to stand as the neuroma in my foot crackled again. Staggering toward the maddening crowd like a newborn giraffe just hit by a truck, a smile came to my face. The truth really does hurt!

3

Everything Old is New Again

We shall not cease from exploration, and
the end of all our exploring will be to arrive where we started
and know the place for the first time.

—T.S. Elliot

March 22nd, 2003
11:00 a.m.

The festivities in the dining hall did not disturb my aura of silence. I knelt down at the donation table to profess my gratefulness to the young woman sitting there as if she owned the place, but no words came out. It was shocking that no air moved through the vocal cords. No sore throat. No fatigue. Just another medical curiosity to consider.

I knew the value of the last ten days but did not have the million dollars handy. Given my inability to socialize I slipped passed the melee to walk the grounds with a full heads-up gaze. Colors were brilliant. Images were sharper than when I arrived. Green blobs were replaced with clear-cut emerald leaves carved against the blue sky. There was a visceral appreciation of the smells in nature.

It was all very clear. ***Wherever there is life there is sensation.*** Scurrying creatures were driven by the multitude of sensations. Plants and animals do not have to think to have these kinds of feelings; their evolutionary habits have built up through eons of time to motivate their present instincts. Information fields use pain and pleasure to tell the muscles and nerves of each critter who and what is friend or foe. Their automated responses reinforce survival behaviors as a feedback loop in consciousness for life to learn and evolve. Good stuff.

The poor human is unknowingly victimized by this primitive inheritance long after we could think for ourselves. Cultures continue to harden their animal ways until a Buddha comes along to say, "watch what you're doing." Ironically, the cravings and aversions to life and death that drive evolution go on to cause all the suffering of the human condition. Looks like psychology and biology are stuck moving the deck chairs around.

Ten days only scratched the surface of the buried recordings pulling my strings. I could not imagine what dread lay in wait in future courses. Never mind what those who were actually traumatized, severely ill, or hardened criminals, would have to endure. But for the mercy of the subconscious mind, how are we even walking around?

March 23rd, 2003
8:00 a.m.

In spite of an otherworldly calm after the storm, the idea of returning for another course any time soon was out of the question. I could not imagine climbing that summit again. The relief of knowing why, what, and where, would do fine for the conceivable future. With my voice coming back online it was nice to be a little sociable on the ride home. I was eager to compare notes after such an intimate shared experience. It was striking that most students stuck to the script, avoiding comparisons. Strange.

Nothing I had learned before was ever good enough. Vipassana had confirmed the partial nature of all other truths. Beneath the psychological minutiae, assorted sensations were at the root of my lifelong resistance and doubt. Countless impulses coerced all my choices for better or worse, and fortunately pushed and prodded me here. So much for free will. Vipassana meditation would finally be good enough.

Professional conferences were never this well managed. Vacations never lived up to the brochure. Nothing in life is ever as good as imagined. Vipassana had surpassed expectations with the blessed certainty of heading in the right direction.

True compassion and empathy would come from deep understanding of this communal fluctuation underlying behavior and emotions. The spectrum from selfish to selfless was seen along the gradient of ignorance to awareness. My next challenge was to forgive society at large, and medical school in particular. They know not what they do.

> "When you know what you want to do
> with the rest of your life, you want the rest of
> your life to begin as soon as possible,"
> —paraphrasing Billy Crystal *When Harry Met Sally*

Goenka opened a door that did not exist anywhere else. If I never took another step on the path, seeing what I saw would suffice for a lifetime. Did this really just happen? Back home I had to confirm this was not just a one-off. I recreated the course schedule as much as possible, bordering on obsession. Early to bed early to rise, thank God the subtle sensations were still there. Whew.

We were told not to expect too much meditating on home turf. Without deep concentration, two hours a day would simply maintain our progress until the next course. I took that parting advice with a grain of salt. We will see. At the course, shifting in place multiplies the habits we were trying to purify so **strong determination** meant sitting as still as possible. At home, bodily movements were permitted as needed. Again, my every thought and sensation screamed to sit still. After forty-two years of driving with the brakes on there was no time to waste.

I could not un-see the storehouse of energy roiling inside. These impurities created all mental and physical suffering that begged for a good house cleaning. The ultimate goal would be accelerated by a constant drip of subconscious stress twenty-four seven. Daily awareness of subtle sensations during routine activities could add up pretty fast.

I was inspired by the Vipassana yogis' whose lucid dreaming was said to be deeper than sleep. That slow leak of unwanted grief sounded pretty good given the two steps back I would take every day. My ulterior motive for hours of reading or entertainment was now a seated opportunity to scan body sensations. This informal meditation supplemented, and at times, supplanted formal sitting. This excuse had worked well enough observing sensations while listening to Goenka's evening discourses.

> *There were no secrets in Vipassana. If you can speak, speak about Vipassana. If you can write, then write about Vipassana. But do not compare your personal experiences in Vipassana. The specific experiences are not important. It is only important to be on the path.*

This new life with Vipassana inspired an unintended sequel to *The Meaning of Health*. The long slow emergence of purpose, love, responsibility and freedom, promised day-to-day rewards of health and happiness. Although full liberation was not realistic in this lifetime, at least I had a working definition of the thing. Thankfully this miraculous journey was truly the destination.

Each day of meditation brought new insights to note. A few pages a day was easy with new context and clarity of all past learning. The guilt of exploiting this gift in a commercial venture felt similar to misusing it to cure back pain. The whole point of the technique was to heal fears and desires over the long haul. While doing my best, there was no point censoring all goals or enforcing morality ahead of schedule. If the sexual impulse ebbs around eighty, I am good with that. Everything in moderation.

***The only measure of progress is how equanimous
you remain in everyday life.***

The opportunity of a lifetime had eased the bittersweet taste of not embodying *The Meaning of Health*. But it was replaced by another bittersweet outlook—admitting this newfound life purpose could not be used as a livelihood. My true nature could not be co-opted for making a living that felt second nature. The path of higher consciousness was not a medical treatment I could deliver to patients. I could not use Vipassana to facilitate healing in others. If eventually I radiated a peaceful presence and sincere empathy in all my interactions, I could live with that.

Equanimity was both the means and the end—evolution's end of the fight-or-flight response. Stunning.

March 24ᵗʰ, 2003

Before the search really took off from Genesis Bookstore, I never forgot an earlier book. *Heading Toward Omega: In Search of the Meaning of the Near-Death Experience* by Kenneth Ring appealed to me after seeing him on a talk show. One psychiatrist opined, "We would cure all our patients if we could reproduce whatever happened to these NDE'ers". I had no interest in the afterlife or psychic experiences, but the transformational change after devastating trauma was fascinating. Instead of the accidental discharge of all suppressed pain with awareness forcibly extricated from the body, Vipassana seemed like a long, slow, near-death experience in the comfort of your own home, without all the blood or the likelihood of actual death. Smart.

10:00 a.m.

Sharpened awareness today is like a magnetic scalpel precisely dissecting the powerful heart muscles. The boldness of the act makes me smile about the arrogance of a surgeon. Feeling my way through the four cardiac chambers I wonder about the sinus node that maintains the heartbeat. I get the immediate hint to back off as the heart starts to flutter, but obviously not soon enough as the subsequent flat-lining lasts way too long. Waiting, waiting, waiting. Note to self: ask the teacher about sudden death in Vipassana. Yikes!

It was a good time to take a break. I was anxious to see how the body behaves at the gym. Feeling energized after ten days of sitting was interesting but losing ten pounds doing nothing was incredible. Half the normal day's calories did not fully explain it. The fat pads under foot were fluffed and refurbished as if wearing new sneakers. There was no end to the intrigue of what purifying the mind meant to the biology.

Grabbing the handles on the seated rower machine, muscles and joints felt like they just had an oil change, lube, and filter. Range of motion was remarkably full and smooth after ten days of inactivity. I clasped my hands behind my back to mindlessly stretch out the shoulders in a yoga pose that the twelve months of Iyengar yoga had not permitted. All of my postures had reached their physical limit that year. This new mindfulness training released whatever blockages restricted the motion. That explains the dramatic contortions of yogis that glide with no muscular or mental resistance.

The whole purpose of exercise flipped upside down from increasing fitness to increasing awareness. The gym would be another way to assess Vipassana progress. Fitness and nutrition would both be demoted to spiritual crosstraining in support of this primary healing modality. Meditation would enhance vitality and longevity more profoundly than weights and veggies alone. This inside information felt like an unfair advantage at the gym. Exercise was another way to appreciate the truth and beauty of nature. Fitness was the welcome side effect.

The curious pulled muscle injury came to mind with new understanding. The wide receiver grabbing his hamstring in mid-stride often had no tissue damage or inflammation. Sport science cannot fully explain this trauma in an activity done thousands of times before. Like the jolt from a seat belt, the rapid muscle extension brings the magnetic restriction into awareness. Larger information fields would also orchestrate the timing and circumstances of the injury. Karma's a bitch.

That's when I heard a crunch in my right knee during a hyperflexion pose of the quadriceps. The visible swelling and locking meant only one thing. But it was weeks to get into the sport clinic for arthroscopic surgery. I got lucky a few times before, but inability to bear weight meant a cartilage tear was inevitable. I used the time to contemplate the difference between Vipassana pain and real-life pain. It was obvious that subtle blockages increase injury-proneness by limiting tissue elasticity. I trusted that embracing the throbbing cartilage with equanimity would encourage healing and repair.

Inspired by the implications, I imagined a Canadian database of healthcare professionals trained in medical Vipassana. I might even go to a doctor once in a while. I would have more faith in my dentist and chiropractor. But a speedy decease and desist reply from the center to my well-intentioned email suggestion was a punch in the gut. A red flag was put on my file. Ouch! My energy bodies knew there was not an entrepreneurial bone in my body.

The admonishment gave me a new appreciation of the unique purity of the teaching and the strict guidelines against commercializing this tradition. Left to my own devices, I would have been tweaking the instructions for 2500 years. I assumed starting an online dating site for meditators was out of the question.

March 29th, 2003
Five o'clock somewhere

That year of sailing had exhausted my interest in beaches, but happy hour was still pretty much mandatory. That was until I returned from the course. Beer and wine suddenly held no appeal, and were even off-putting, like when sick with the flu. Those frosted beers were very ingrained, so it was shocking that alcohol could have quit me so quickly. Even morning coffee was optional. I hoped this unbelievable change transferred to the rest of my life.

Buddha included the mind as a sixth sense because thoughts and emotions were felt like senses in the body. We cannot choose our thoughts any more than our sensations that pop up unasked. A lifetime of memory patterns constantly informs us how to feel and what to think about it. Instinctual reactions multiply by the day to prevent us becoming wise in old age. I was sold on the observation of sensation as the one thing that heals everything. The presumed mechanisms of traditional therapies were now undermined by this inadvertent facilitation of sitting with feelings. The mind put the pain in there and only the mind can let it out.

Attention on the body must work the same way in non-meditators' everyday life, albeit not as strongly. This explains how mindful diet and fitness improves wellbeing beyond the nutrients and the exercise. Alternatively, mindless gossip and distraction interferes with the effects of massage and physical therapies. Awareness is the secret ingredient to relieve suffering at any level.

All the new treatments for post-traumatic stress, phobias, and obsessive-compulsive disorders facilitate the patient facing fears without reacting in a controlled environment. It was amazing what intuitive psychologists and creative docs figured out. It became obvious now that like medication, all variety of braces and pain-relief gizmos conspire to push the root cause of pain out of sight, only to sprout up again later. Alternative medicine and Eastern healing would also be less effective when used symptomatically or mindlessly.

But it is clear that circumstances can only trigger what is already there. When we accept the stress-proneness of our repressed fears, we can take all of the responsibility and none of the blame for illness and injury. Happiness, love, and wellbeing are inside jobs, so external seeking only gets you so far. Research agrees that increasing purpose, love, responsibility and freedom are deep cleaning for health. Every step on the path enhances the biological set point for preventing and coping with inevitable challenges.

April 12th, 2003

Do not believe anything because the Buddha said so,
because your teacher said so, or because your scripture said so.
Only believe what you can verify within
your own direct experience.

Goenka tells the story of a young child refusing to eat his delicious rice pudding as there is a black stone in it. The mother says, "No baby, it is cardamom, you will like it. If not, put it aside and enjoy the rest."

"No!" The boy throws his dish on the floor.

Do not be like the child. If there is anything unacceptable in the teaching, leave it alone and enjoy the rest. Later, you might try again.

That was reassuring, but for the fact my black stone was the foundational core of the teaching. Everything ***changes***. Each meditation session ended abruptly with Goenka's enthusiastic chanting in Pali. ***Annica, annica! Change, change!*** Familiar with being an outsider, I assumed I was the only one unable to join in the silent revelry.

Yes, I recognized that sensations are constantly changing. I got that. The same fluctuating essence showed up in biology, physics, and psychology. Cells are continually being renewed, subatomic particles constantly sparkle in and out of existence, and life circumstances need endless adjustments. Buddha taught that we are literally feeling the smallest bits of subatomic matter, kalapas in Pali. I had my doubts that our nervous system was capable of perceiving trillions of quantum particles in the blink of an eye. Also, ten years of reading about change had gotten me nowhere fast.

The whole self-help industry sprang up because people cannot change that easily. The possibility of healing intractable habits was far more exciting than the current flux of sensations. This purification utilizing the changing sensations was only a reality for those practicing Vipassana. And even with that, real-life change was not that forthcoming. The lack of change in my life put a damper on rejoicing for flowing particles.

Our biology, psychology, and physics were pretty hardwired. But I had faith that awareness and equanimity could slowly soften, melt, and evaporate the suffering of these scientific realities. With conflicted resentment, my own selfish chant was *dissolve, release,* and *heal.*

Since I am venting, the repetitive warning of playing games with sensations did not resonate either. Are others really squandering this occasion to avoid certain sensations and revel in others? We can do that back home. This was the safest place to face both addictions and aversions. I didn't care how much it hurt or how long it took. Let's do this.

> **Do not identify yourself with the sensations.**
> **Why would you attach yourself to something**
> **so fleeting and insubstantial?**

To not identify with something so ephemeral as subtle sensations sounded like pop psychology. I did not see how identity was related to sensations. I never thought of my sense of self as a conscious choice. I assumed purification would take care of that anyway. Admittedly, all my old injuries that resurfaced in meditation were my injuries; I guess I identified with them.

Another sticking point for me was the second key teaching of anatta (no-self). A universal teaching, I never understood how exactly the personal self was an illusion. It was exciting that precise observation promised to naturally lessen these attachments to the personality beyond my understanding. I did trust that we were indeed accessing the subconscious mind. But I took it on faith that witnessing sensations actually purified the mind of negativities.

It must be semantics. The words or the context rubbed me the wrong way. But things seemed to be working. Hopefully, staying calm with sensations would be enough for now. Too many blind spots from too many books meant I had a lot of unlearning to do. Whatever was blocking my understanding was encoded in the same sensations that would eventually burn away like everything else. I had to put all these black stones aside to enjoy the rest.

April 20th, 2003

I did take the moral precepts for granted. Lying, stealing, and killing did not seem an urgent concern at the course. Sexual misconduct and intoxication needed further clarification. In the context of purification, the higher purpose of good behavior was not to indulge ingrained fears and desires. Bad behavior meant multiplying the self-punishing habits of greed, lust, and guilt. It appeared that the origin of morality was based on purifying one's mind. Being kind to others was a benevolent side effect. Fascinating!

Either way, it was counterproductive to mindlessly react to animal urges when investing so much time meditating for peace. Relative decency got me in the door, but I had the vague notion that there was more nuance to the story of virtues.

May 17th, 2003

Scanning sensations became a pleasant way to ease into sleep without tossing and turning. But over the long hot summer, the stress of life brought out the stark contrast between vibrations while sitting and day-to-day worries. It was easier to sit through physical pain than walk around with gnawing concerns. The sound of my savings circling the drain began to drown out the silence that was fading fast in the rear-view mirror.

The tepid response of publishers and editors to *Meaning* was demoralizing. I had no inclination toward self-promotion without the OK of at least one other human. The dream now was only to support my new contemplative lifestyle. As magical as it was on the mat, the power of observation did not promise miracles on the street.

Better to never find the Dhamma,
than find it and not pursue it.

June 1ˢᵗ, 2003

With the high from the course receding, the mounting life strain was stronger than the waning alcohol craving. Stressful thoughts were still harder to surrender than physical strain, so I excused a few cold brews over the summer. I trusted that all cravings will eventually ebb on their own accord so why deprive myself on this middle path. I did not see any definitive effect on the meditation. The slight buzz and mild guilt of that rationalization only shifted the timing of when to sit. Admittedly, a drinking game of counting the beers until numb to sensations was ill-advised.

This low point was enough to consider another round of Vipassana. At least my knee settled down without the need for surgical intervention. With increasing awareness, things would feel worse before they feel better. Disappointment with not taking full advantage of my near-life experience was enough to book another course.

4

BODY BY BUDDHA

June 15th, 2003

The Buddha's renegade integrity was impressive. He had refused the designations of the highest attainments from all of the Indian spiritual traditions of the time. They were not good enough. In the peace and tranquility, something was still bothering him. It only took few weeks under the Bodhi tree to realize the subtlest impulses of the mind-body phenomenon that create pain and suffering. Complete liberation to him meant total relief of mental impurities at the essence of the human condition. The right type of concentration and awareness meant a different type of enlightenment. Liberation included the cleansing of all negativities in addition to the transcendental peace of other traditions.

Vipassana was a universal non-sectarian approach to realize the ultimate nature of everything by deeply knowing oneself. Purposely avoiding the contentious words *God* and *soul*, Buddha referred to the essence of existence as Dhamma. For me, the technique was already reconciling the limits of science and psychology. The partial truths in medicine could not be fleshed out using the same linear approach. Even spiritual aphorisms and new-age clichés made more sense in the context of their original source.

Always keep your back and neck straight implied some anatomical importance to the process while avoiding any specific landmarks. Meditating on subtle sensations was a physical form of introspection that utilized gravity through the postures and the supports. The tighter the posture and the harder the floor invited a keener awareness of the inner turbulence. Although any comfortable sitting posture was permitted, it appeared that the lotus position with minimal cushioning was most effective to coax subconscious vibrations into the light of awareness.

Yoga postures similarly use gravity to wring out the soft tissue around joints from every possible angle. With progress, less pain and resistance in tendons and ligaments allow more advanced postures. Alternatively, the stiffness of aging suggests an accumulation of electromagnetic adhesions that underlie an accelerated musculoskeletal degeneration.

I knew levels of consciousness to be the inner development of identity and worldview. Equanimity in daily life was the new measure of progress. How defensive, contentious, and easily offended, reflected the work left to do. Vipassana offered a practical way to strengthen one's character and weaken one's faults. I would have to double check whether my impatience for maturity and civility is in the same ballpark of craving enlightenment.

Accepting progress on its own time was based on the unknown stock of subconscious conditioning. It was easier to accept the idea of karma as inherited habits that primed the pump for the current personality to supercharge the patterns. All I ever needed to respect the rules was good reasoning. Being able to witness emerging awareness through purification was more than I ever expected. I was happy to hunker down and enjoy the ride with a knowing faith and an active hope.

July 3rd, 2003
Merritt, BC
Second Course

Day Two

There are none of the facial sensations to absorb my attention this time around. This reveals the difficulties of holding the focus on the simple flow of the breath even for a minute. Each day of Anapana narrows the area of concentration above the upper lip. The smaller the target the sharper the mind for later exploration and dissection. I take that to heart by narrowing down to a single point at the tip of my lip. Everything to the extreme. I ignore the construction work shaking the ground, until I realize we are not anywhere near a construction site.

Desperate for more, I did not easily accept sitting through the same intro instructions. I soon realize many details are missed the first time around between being lost in thought, Goenka's accent, and perfectly timed coughs and sneezes. Plus, the meaning of the same words change with the deepening of experience. A hint of the nature of concentration comes as the audio sounds as if I am sitting in a deep hole in the ground.

Day Three

I miss the old laser face tag that did most of the concentrating for me. Steady attention remains difficult without slightly forcing the breath. At best, focus is sustained simultaneously with streams of consciousness. The first-day thoughts are mundane. The next two days are filled with agonizing regrets and worries. Excruciating shame and doubt feel worse than when the events actually happened. By magnifying every detail, meditation reveals how much of pain is spontaneously repressed just to survive. I had previously escaped this difficult part of Anapana during the psychotic facial. There is no way I will have the same power of touch as I had last time during Vipassana.

Vipassana Day Four

The technique is very forgiving of ignorance and mistakes. Immediately after the Vipassana Day rituals and teaching, swarms of bees overwhelm the body. No idea how I reached this deep level of perception. It does prove the stark difference between meditating at home and after four days of Anapana, however inept.

Water boils whenever you get around to turning on the stove without judgment or penalty. The higher awareness that cleanses the mind simply bides its time until you decide to show up. This gives me permission to forgive myself and accept the lifelong accumulations for lack of diligence. I rely more and more on the basic instructions whenever I hit any roadblocks. It is new for me to appeal to a higher power but if I could have done this myself, I would have done it a long time ago.

Day Five

I am working my way through the body with a little more maturity. Over-enthusiasm transmutes into a hurry-up-and-wait mentality. The dissecting probe is an invisible finger of exceptional dexterity in tiny areas.

Kneecaps are red hot coals, and femurs white hot pokers that will take lifetimes to cool. Learning my lessons from the previous course, I leave the organs to fester in the background with trust that some part of the mind is keeping tabs on the situation.

Day Seven

Hours and hours of cycling around the body, the top of my skull endures twenty pounds of pressure before deep inner rumblings. The shaky crown now crumbles and deflates down to the base of the skull, leaving an anencephalic nightmare in its wake.

I intuit a vague outline of a blind spot on the right side of my neck that slowly balloons out a few inches. The ghostly growth blocks out any sensation as it swells over the shoulder below and the temple above. This photographic negative is billowing above and threatening to engulf the flattened skull. I fear the advancing electrical silence obliterating my mind. As it begins its decent, I say my goodbyes in the fifty-fifty chance of disappearing for good. I recall the Vipassana ritual taking refuge in Triple Gem. Asking for protection in the truth of the Dhamma, qualities of the Buddha, the power of the Sangha (historic vipassana community) comes easy when facing stark uncertainty.

The vacant blob oozes down my dismantled forehead, vanishing everything in its wake. It passes over my eyes in the front and occiput in back. Life and mind are strangely spared another day. The cone of silence brings new tranquility as it consumes my neck, chest and torso. Absolutely riveted with no noticeable breath or track of time, the wherewithal comes to scan the missing body above and the leading edges of the rolling apocalypse below. The stealthy jellyfish envelops my pelvis and legs, pulling and tugging before slipping off the end of my toes like a pair of nylons.

All body activity is radio silent, imperceptible, gone. Attention cycles up and down a memory silhouette of a body with lightning speed and precision. Gradually, the finest perceptible particles emerge from the ether like fingerprint dust to reveal the bodily details.

Again, a flowering presence arises on the same point on the C-spine to blossom up and back to devour the body leaving another blank canvass. The fifth time in the hour, snake skins repeatedly peel off the feet followed each time by a yet finer powdery essence bubbling up to color in the lines.

Out of the blackness arises a wet brick, encasing the eye sockets, forehead, and skull. The cement block hardens to embed itself in the bone with corners protruding. It tugs facial muscles into an involuntary smile. The solid rock vibrates and quivers before eventually crumbling and passing over the body like thick lava without the heat. As before, the formidable brick repeatedly forms above before melting over the body with changing consistency from honey to porridge to free-flowing liquid, leaving nothing in its place.

A fine silken wardrobe emerges again and again from the depths. Meaningless and random are not the words that come to mind. The ten-pound eye mask returns for the long haul as the tip of the tailbone is violently grumbling.

The strange bedfellows of a translucent body and an opaque brick lodged in my forehead took over for the night, compelling me to grab a seat in the hallway. After an hour of pummeling I am shooed away by the student manager. I had not tested the rule—lights out at ten—before. Involuntarily, I stay awake in bed for a couple more hours as things played themselves out.

Metta Day Ten

The last couple of days bring an unearthly peace and joy. The sensory deprivation is enough to stop trying to figure things out. It does feel like layers and layers of the subconscious sludge is being flushed away. It's a wonder I never get headaches as this surreal paperweight continues to weigh on my skull.

Day Eleven

Before the ride home a documentary plays about Vipassana being taught to inmates at high security prisons. I cannot see as my eye lids are too heavy to open. The sacrum harnesses a bag of furious snakes that elongates up through the stomach. Flapping into the lungs, my jaw is forced open to exhale the thundering cloud over a few minutes. The movie ends as a balloon is tethered between the tailbone and crown before expanding and enveloping the body.

The wild antics of the subconscious seem to show an orderly precision. There was a definite disconnect with the teaching that says all emanations are random and meaningless. All spiritual traditions talk about reality as an illusion, but at least Vipassana acknowledged we are still responsible for the apparent truth of day-to-day life. ***Don't leave your day job.***

Our senses cannot perceive the ultimate truth of life. I get that. But it was not easy to drop the long-sought meaning of health and happiness. Giving up these attachments makes sense for the purposes of the practice itself. In terms of cleansing the mind during meditation, yes, just let it go.

Understanding this theatre as a waking dream, of course, I was happy to relieve myself of it. While the mind is not to be trusted, I thought I could do two things at once. Fascination with the mind-and-body relationship would not stop me from observing objectively. Having said that, I was alert to the fact that every thought is also a byproduct of the passing BS.

It was the agony of leaving the place that really hurt. It was inconceivable to waste sacred operating time by socializing on Shock Absorber Day (day ten). It took ten grueling days just to prep. I was literally ripped out of surgery with my guts still on the table to travel on day eleven. Elbows-deep in psychic surgery, I could barely contain a full-blown temper tantrum on the ride home, resenting having to stitch myself up on the highway. So much for equanimity.

There was no guarantee this golden opportunity will come again anytime soon. The guilt over sulking was two giant steps back. Equanimity in everyday life was more difficult than in the protective cocoon of meditation. Hopefully, the gratitude and compassion were true enough to keep my head above water.

On the three-hour traffic jam home, I considered the many authors and books that supported me. Many wrote of psychic or transcendent experiences in childhood that gave them a head start on the path to higher consciousness. It would be interesting to hear from someone who started from scratch. With Vipassana as my wingman, I embraced my role as a blue-collar Buddha, lunch box in hand, clocking the long hours. No extra sensory perception. No guiding angels. No spontaneous combustion.

My good fortune was finding Vipassana when I did—being ready, willing, and able to see the value. So few are interested. Less have the time. Even less are committed. Compassion came from knowing our common condition. It was definitely a responsibility to pursue and share this truth in an accessible way.

"To anyone who hears of enlightenment,
you will never be satisfied with anything less."
—Buddha

I just wanted to be part of society, but Vipassana had slingshot me right past the crowd. The road less travelled carved a detour to the further shore. While I desperately needed a few extra days, I could not conceive of a twenty-day sit, mostly because of the double dose of Anapana. Excruciating guilt and regret were gut-wrenching distractions that made any concentration a miracle. Add to that the punishing fatigue and fierce head pressures. Blistering headaches and rampant electrical shorts were considerably worse with no opportunity for relief by scanning the body.

Racking my brain, I could not see any conscious choice in determining a sense of self. I did not see a relationship between subtle sensations and the personal self. If identity was merely a mental program, it would lessen on its own accord. If the self-sense was somehow cobbled together from subconscious sensations, I would happily kick the habit as it comes up. I never expected to make sense of the *no-self* teaching until and unless the *I* literally passed away. That I would like to see.

The spiritual goals of meditation took a back seat to the promises of incremental healing. Yet, I accepted that thought and sensation are mysteriously observed within a subjectivity unbounded by spacetime. If and when all experience ceases, awareness would still feel like the familiar me for the moment. The genius of the technique was in the progressive understanding long before the absolute truth of full liberation, just by showing up.

My attachment to results did not allow me to enjoy Metta day chit-chat in preparation to face the world. The nature of concentration itself was elusive, realized only in retrospect by the decompression sickness that occurred after speaking. Talking too soon or too fast triggered painful cramps in my fingers of all things. It also yanked on my guts in a nauseous attempt to shut me up. Maybe it wasn't just me being a baby.

The physicality of the process felt more like an active doing than passive observing. The constant riptide compelled a sense of swimming upstream rather than the promised surfing and sailing. Navigating the magnetically charged surfaces and the electrical interiors made strained breathing inevitable.

Unearthing a lifetime of injuries made me rethink the karmic aspects of unfortunate circumstances. Electromagnetic blockages would decrease tissue resilience that predispose injury in targeted locations. There is something deeper than angles and forces to explain soft-tissue tears and fractures. Incidents and accidents remain buried in flesh along with disappointments and regret, waiting to be relived in the clear light of awareness.

I was bursting to share these experiences and insights. But there was none of that urgency in others. Admittedly, you cannot really compare with people being all over the board, at different starting points, differing views, and proceeding at their own pace. But the reason given of envy or self-pity did not resonate. No one was jealous hearing the Buddha's experience. I could not square that with the encouragement to speak or write of Vipassana. All of the officially sanctioned Vipassana books so far had stuck to the same script as the teachers. When advising patients, I took pleasure in painting as many metaphors as possible until one of them clicked: Just breathe.

I agreed with Goenka that the only satisfying answers will come from within. The teachers were trained to keep the focus on the basics and prevent students from falling down their own rabbit holes. Students were encouraged to sit with their questions as long as they could before indulging the craving to ask. Five-minute noon interviews were strictly for technical concerns, avoiding forays into hypotheticals and the theoretical. Anyway, this teacher reassured me that my anatomical knowledge was unavoidable and acceptable for dissections. She had not heard of anyone dropping dead of cardiac arrest during meditation. Good to know.

Vipassana was ruining me for everything else. In a good way, vacations, entertainment, and hobbies became a temporary respite or intentional distraction. With a future life of perpetual growth, I had gotten everything I wanted.

Never make a show of meditation in public.
Yet maintain awareness with eyes open.
Continuity is the secret of success.

Back home I felt the distinct edges of concrete encasing my skull above the eyes. The hardened block turned into Styrofoam, before melting slowly down my back each day. Mimicking every headache in the book, I wondered why I never had them but for the rare fever. Contemplative life became a priority for preventive health and longevity. Coffee-shop reading maintained the continuous drip of organic dark energy.

Back at the gym a new level of mindfulness turned weight training into genuine yoga. Breathing right through muscles improved structure and function. Feeling the full thickness of muscle allowed surprising relaxation and alignment in poses and stretching. The new equanimity quickly overcame the deep tendon reflexes. Lengthening muscle was more than physical pulling. Awareness itself could explain the increased range of motion and injury prevention. It was obvious that the deeper the mindfulness the more influence awareness had on everyday life.

Fitness had always been about efficiency. Get in and get out. Ironically, reading *Very Slow Resistance Training* would help speed things up. Using half the weight and one third the speed allowed tension to build at each point along the range of motion. This avoided the common cheating of using acceleration to throw the weight up and allowing gravity to drop the weight down. Awareness alone would maximize muscle fibre recruitment and strength, without bulking up.

Strong determination in the gym gave a whole new incentive to feeling the burn. Equanimity with exercise was just another way of discharging the subconscious debris. Intentionally facing the pain could account for the mood-elevating benefits of fitness long before the endorphins kicked in. These mental flow states make possible the transcendent athletics that break the four-minute barriers in all sports. Buddha and Einstein agreed, mind precedes matter.

Mindful exercise meant you actually had to be present to get results. It was also therapy by confronting pain now to avoid suffering later. The pervasive phone and TV distractions were obvious impediments to holistic fitness goals. A new relationship with the body came from killing two birds with one workout. I credited my inherent laziness for finding ways of working smarter. A higher purpose for all physical enjoyment was found by paying more attention.

*A problem cannot be fixed from the same
level that created it.*

—Einstein

The last few decades of mind-body medicine had connected purpose, love, freedom, and responsibility with health, happiness, and longevity. Pretty good stuff for objective science. Vipassana shows more precisely how consciousness effects the physiology. Attitudes, beliefs, and identity influence metabolism, stress, and genetic expression as well as values, lifestyles, and choices. Emotions and behaviors then act as the feedback mechanism that multiply the mental habit patterns. Healing is difficult because the same person that created the illness is the one trying to heal it.

There was always something missing in medicine. It was the patient. Their subjective reality was the key determinant of health and wellbeing. Granted, the mechanics of symptoms are eased with mechanical treatments, but emotions and molecules are both objects in consciousness influenced by awareness.

The germ theory of infection always seemed incomplete. Cancer was not just about mutated genes. Inflammatory conditions and life-threatening allergies were not entirely explained by external triggers. The molecular mechanisms that we suppress or stimulate do not address why one person gets sick, the unique severity of their symptoms, or how well they respond to treatment. Germs, genes, and biochemistry could be seen in the greater context of consciousness.

I learned early on that symptoms do not always match the test results. Pristine joints can be painful while battered old cartilage functions well. Back and knee surgeries were becoming less and less popular as the research acknowledged the conflicting results. Vipassana shows how mutual belief, trust, and faith in healers and treatments create a placebo effect stronger than the therapy itself, without knowing which is which. Likewise, the nocebo effect influences the popular symptoms through cultural hypnosis and fearmongering media.

The list of psychosomatic disease had been steadily increasing by default from conflicting and confusing treatment results. I had no problem taking the leap that all diseases are psychosomatic in the sense of originating in the habit patterns in consciousness. Emotions and perceptions in time and space are as electromagnetic as the molecular body. Consciousness is the final frontier of medicine that will take health and happiness to the next level.

A tinge of guilt came from co-opting Vipassana to confirm my long-suffering intuitions of health and illness. I would surrender it all in a minute to become a genuine, loving, and peaceful person. I had to trust in the nature of purification until I knew for myself. But I had a strong sense that this profound path offered the most noble healing.

The climb toward purpose, love, freedom, and responsibility had plateaued. Vipassana had thrown me a rope to continue this higher purpose. Compassion would come from seeing the same yearning in others no matter the route. Responsibility from being ready, willing, and able. The freedom from suffering inspired the journey. They were all resonant qualities from the same benevolent practice.

The scientific technique of the Buddha shines light into the shadows beyond the purview of medicine, therapy or self-study. Overcoming our child and animal inheritance would vastly improve the human condition. Equanimity became my new favorite synonym for health and happiness, however bulky.

5

Angels and Demons

September 10th, 2003
Merritt, BC
Serving Sati

I was more prepared for the beatdown from my second course than I was for the humbling impressions that it left on me. I had to accept that penetrating fireworks did not instantly translate into explosive life change. But the awe of accessing this truth sustained my passion for the clarity and direction in life. I was never outwardly ambitious. Vipassana was my success. I was never more suited for any other endeavor. The subtitle for *The Meaning of Health* was *The Experience of a Lifetime,* and this would be mine.

There was support at home in terms of weekly group meditations, the Vipassana Research Institute (VRI), and an online bookstore exclusive to VRI publishing. I signed up for the "Daily Words of the Buddha" emails to keep the good vibrations going. It was reassuring that the Buddha mentioned ***inner fervor*** on the path; ***Once hearing of enlightenment, you will never be satisfied with anything less.*** This fire in the belly gave me some cover for any obsessive compulsion.

Volunteering was the lifeblood of the centers. Serving was solicited more than donations. The karmic merit from ten days of selflessly caring for others outweighed one moment of swiping the credit card. Less clear was how serving a course could advance awareness more than sitting a few courses. Nevertheless, I was eager to give back and immerse myself in culinary loving-kindness.

There would be plenty of face time with the teacher. I was sure there were more secrets about both practice and theory. The courses were said to be designed in a way that the teaching did not get ahead of the student's experience. Of course, I felt that my freestyling was way ahead of the theory. A few official Vipassana books had not revealed much more than the introductory discourses. I was not yet qualified to sit this advanced eight-day Satipatthana course, but I hoped to peek behind the curtain during the discourses and talks with the teacher while serving a less hectic course.

One teacher assured me that we were given enough basic information to cover the entire path with no big surprises ahead. I had concerns that between ignorance and eagerness I may veer off course. I was mildly shocked at the audio presentation for servers on how to deal with pressures and conflicts of working together. Conflicts? This was a Vipassana center. A sacred space, supportive atmosphere, with shared purpose should be enough to keep us in line. I mentioned this unknowingly to a stunned teacher-in-training who thought I was kidding. I wasn't. He laughed again when I asked about the qualifications and spiritual attainments of assistant teachers. After seven years of devoted commitment, those who were invited into teacher training were not screened with a mental status exam. OK.

I was still defiant about the persistent chanting of *change*. I could not articulate this cognitive dissonance other than denying that sensations were actually quantum particles. That's when they kicked me out.

I don't know how she knew, but some old student who sat on the board had complained that rookie servers cannot listen to the veteran discourses. Listening outside on the sidewalk below a window just felt wrong after a few evenings. I hadn't heard anything new anyway and wondered when the advanced part kicked in.

Day Five

I appreciate the extended meditation hours between kitchen duties without the dreaded Anapana. I am grateful for the raging fires and precision dissections that strengthen my commitment. As awareness inadvertently passes through the inner ear, a high-fidelity tympani sounds up and down for an extended engagement. Time to cut up the veggies.

Day Six

With a magnetic fist, I physically wring out the intestines like a sponge. The thin muscular walls were indeed mostly nerves known as a second brain. Lifetimes of tension waft through an open back that had unzipped from the skull to the sacrum. Hour after hour, layers of broken glass sting as they peel off the torso, gradually crushing down to fine sparkling dust. Time to make salad dressing.

Day Seven

Breathing easily inside and outside, the neural anatomy lights up like a Christmas tree. The whole translucent body then balloons out two feet before forcefully shrink-wrapping the limbs down to pencils. Oddly, I become entombed by a bony exoskeleton that paralyzes my scanning ability. It is a good time to quit and prepare for next morning's breakfast.

Day Eight

Six hours of daily Vipassana, even without Anapana, sharpens the mind notably finer than at home. Familiar grandiose plans for the future emerge after a week, contrasting sharply with the crimpling doubts and anxiety at the beginning. It is amazing how layers of negativity clear away like the clouds, allowing a sunnier disposition to shine.

Resisting the key insight of change was of my own making. Too many books with too many perspectives had polished my projections beyond recognition. How exactly pleasure was part of suffering along with the insight that there is no-self would take even more time. I did trust that continued practice would clarify all. I was sure that morality and equanimity were also more layered and profound. But my doubts that the nervous system could sense subatomic creation were still hanging out there like a big matzo ball.

September 21, 2003

Regret and worry were always more uncomfortable than unemotional knee pain. At a course, nothing was more agonizing than reliving the excruciating minutia of every past conversation and circumstance over the decades. The sensitivity from an increasingly porous subconscious filter made all suffering worse before it got better. The good news was that subjective symptoms should be more amenable to healing than hardened disability.

What was certain was that equanimity and awareness do not transfer well to daily life. I was not mindful enough to get out in front of every mindless thought and behavior. There was a small window of opportunity between cravings and the sheer force of will to drop the sensations driving the vices. The guilt from not taking full advantage of that six-week alcohol sabbatical was worse than drinking the beer and wine itself.

November 5th, 2003
Third course

Hopefully, third time's a charm when it comes to understanding concentration. In the first course I was amused and distracted with facial Armageddon. By the second course, I was not even aware of the deeper states of mind or how they aided Vipassana.

Day Two

Thinking ahead to powerful dissections, I proactively isolate the pinpoint tip of the upper lip. I look past constant doubts and fears to the quiet background without much luck. Somehow, through perpetual negativities, some bits of attention hang onto the breath.

I notice that the breath continues in line with the gut to account for the lack of hunger during a course. Every bite of food is prominently felt in the stomach. Unlike generic mindfulness training, the physical effects of this tradition are immediate and impressive. With any luck, it's a lot easier to watch what I'm eating back at home.

Day Three

Still leaning on the breath, I cannot ignore the brewing vibrations begging for attention throughout the rest of the body. My head is consumed in a billowing vortex, while brilliant white light flickers from under the eyelids. The right hamstring is threatening the same spasms that routinely woke me up as a teenager. Vipassana Day is anticipated and welcomed like an old friend.

Day Six

Negotiating the pain in previous courses taught me that there was no need for aggressive tactics. Scanning the surface, I wonder if deeper sensations eventually rise through the skin on their own, defeating the purpose of surgical incision. After thunder clouds roll through on day five, a half dozen railway rails have been haphazardly impaling me from behind. Like a ragdoll, the crisscrossing iron rods string me up for unbearable hours.

Each step deeper brings more dexterity for wrapping around fingers and toes. Dominating forces hold me bolt upright in an ever tightening half-lotus position. Time and space stretch out and double back to their own devices. Breathing settles down in lockstep with slowing thought processes. Without the need for oxygen, the breath flows into the lungs under ambient pressure.

Facial muscles mimic assorted emotions on the whim of swirling energies. Interesting. Coughing and choking from a thin wire garrote chiseling into the larynx explains the speech impediment after each course. Throat chakra? A vice grip on the forehead rocks violently for hours until entire crown splits open to a raging inferno. Without any heat, I fan through the magnetic flames with waves of attention. I watch transfixed at what can only be years of emotional kindling burning away.

Day Nine

By day nine the steel shafts melt into serrated scrap metal, tearing through my shoulder blades as an intolerable deformed mess. Tears coming down, I am cautious not to antagonize the situation, but each tiny breath inflames the simmering mass. My shirt is soaked from the rock wall exertion, except that the rockface is climbing me.

Over an afternoon, the right leg repeatedly morphs from a throbbing cement block to flowing lava that stops dead at the midline. By the end of each hour the magma fires reduce to raw embers of spinal cord nerves. Legs and back are surprisingly revitalized after days in the burning rubble.

*Goenka's voice drifts through the chaos, **you must pay your debts.** YES! It is absolutely my pleasure to actually do something, anything to* *forgive myself, to redeem myself, but from what? From an ignorant life of inertia? Now with the ways and the means, I owe it to myself and others. The only way out is through.*

Finally, the purpose of med school is seen as preparation for this healing institute of higher learning. As gross impurities evaporate, bone and muscle fade away as a subtler anatomy emerges in its place. It is comforting to think of a non-judgmental, non-punitive spiritual path that is electromagnetically neutral. Pain and suffering are the self-imposed harm of mindless reactions to cravings and aversion, plus centuries of inherited bad deeds. Fascinating to see how it all got anthropomorphized.

Anyone I know would be in the psych ward after a few days of navgating this nightmare. Upsetting lifelike dreams continue the work overnight. No wonder a few students scream bloody murder before leaving each course on day two or day six.

February 4th, 2004

I am aware of sitting upright until the realization that my physical head and torso are reclined a few inches back. The sense of myself is leaning outside of the body. To test out this mini out-of-body experience (OBE) I sit back to align with the body before leaning forward again a few times. Yes, I suppose it is possible for awareness to drift outside of the body. Experience does not actually take place in the body but in a field of awareness that only correlates loosely with the body. The mistake is only realized after a peek from the outside in. I am not quite floating above the operating room table watching my own surgery, but it's enough to make the point.

I am so grateful for this controlled safe exploration of inner nature rather than an inadvertent metaphysical trauma. Without this long slow learning curve how else to sanely interpret these frightening ordeals. I recall early on being upside down at the level of my abdomen. I opened an eye to confirm the immobile body, ceiling below and floor above.

That explains the spiritual teaching that we are not in our heads. Intentionally leaning out proves it is not the physical body that is ballooning out, tearing open, or morphing into various shapes. The energy body contorts itself to maximize surface area in order to release eons of repressed information. The same ethereal sensations are mistaken as the mundane experience in everyday life. Symptoms of illness and meditation are the same ephemeral feelings in differing degrees and awareness. If everything is subjective, then all suffering can be eased through awareness alone.

After meditation, I noticed a drop of dried blood centered on my chin. I washed it away without finding a cut or a blemish. That reminded me of the religious stigmata in psychosis, possession, or extreme stress. There was no definitive cause of spontaneous bleeding or proof that it leaked out through the sweat glands. But *sweating* blood was definitely a thing under the right conditions. The right conditions evidently are intense electromagnetic frequencies informed by the cultural subconscious. It suited me fine if all diverse religious tales originated from one universal mystical experience.

March 1ˢᵗ, 2004

The unfurled spinal muscles and melted steel had eased my longstanding upper back tension. Still, mounting pressure on both shoulder blades is reminiscent of teenage angst. Localized buds are now protruding from the inner spine of each scapula.

A physical presence is hovering above and behind me like a heavy rucksack. Making my way around the massive load, I inch along the ridges of the bony blades recalling my anatomy. Shock and disbelief are understatements in the face of anatomically correct wings precipitating a foot above and three below out of this field of dreams. The familiar pressure is dramatized by inch-thick bones branching into Hollywood-style limbs of flight. Ridiculous!

OK breathe. Impersonal, meaningless, impermanent—these appendages simply represent eons of collective mythology in their full-feathered glory. Certainly not personal, how literal the collective consciousness lives to sustain the various traditions. These things are heavy and all I can think about is healing decades of back strain. Stunned and awed, I make my way around the body for some semblance of normalcy.

Even alone, this is too embarrassing to share. It behooves me to pour on the equanimity and nonattachment. Yes, all in the mind but as physical as anything else. I am happy to replace the physical burden with the new mental burden. It is enough just to embrace the method in the madness—random, essenceless, choiceless. It was easy for Buddha—who had seen it all before—to ignore the pesky details as mere distractions to liberating peace. Intrigued by the historical drama, I forgive my naivete as a tiny step back. Fascinating.

Coming back to earth was easy with growing financial and career uncertainty. I never know if I will ever get back to the center, so I booked my fourth course before crawling back to Winnipeg, dragging myself back to work, and basically, going backwards.

April 7th, 2004
Fourth course
Day Two

Focus is strong again on the first day of Anapana. By day two, past and future replay ad nauseum, more agonizing than any physical pain. The endless rehashing and redoing of conversations is unbearable. Shame and humiliation about life gnaw away for hours without end.

You cannot choose your sensations and you cannot choose your thoughts. There is no escape.

Forcing the breath is still an issue, fatigue and pressure are annoying, and ideas of a long course are out of the question. The background tension is building rapidly without any way to release it. It is hard enough holding attention for one minute on the breath without the body being crushed. I consider secretly scanning the body occasionally to defuse the ticking timebomb.

Day Three

Subtler sensations at the lip magnify the now tiny stream of the breath. The breath flow goes to trickle as a strong magnetic thread holds the attention at the tip of the lip. Tight focus on a teeny spot is a steep escalator into the depths where thought is partially paralyzed. Appetite suppression and early satiety reveal real physiological change that come from passing looks at the gut.

Day Seven

The body disappears into a perpetual energy flow. Effort is minimized before being overtaken completely by automated reflexes not unlike a continuous sneeze, hiccup, or sexual climax. The bowl of pelvic nerves dissects out to fan up around the hip bones like a cobra. This throws fuel on the femurs already like glowing coals. The last twenty minutes of each session is a tortuous negotiation with pain. I can't tell if deconditioning the mind increases the tolerance for pain or better yet, eventually there is less pain to tolerate, or both.

Day Eight

For hours, the fuming crown shows itself as the final incinerator for the whole nervous system. It makes sense that the skin is searing along with all branching nerves given their similar embryonic origins. I cannot fathom the electrical debris scraping the nerves in patients with multiple sclerosis or ALS. By day eight the brain itself ignites into a lava flow, crawling down the back like an Indian headdress.

The sheer volume of this submerged hell is as mindboggling as its blissful ignorance in daily life. I am forced to consider past lives as my personal stress cannot account for this amount of retribution. Just as genetic inheritance is informed by the evolutionary past, a historical cast of characters must fuel the individual subconscious.

Doubt and negativity live on the surface while positivity and generosity bubble up toward the end of the week. The same life concerns from day two return in the peacefulness of day eight without triggering any upset. That is the promise of eventual freedom. Liberated beings remain unperturbed with only wisps of normal human emotions. Endless mental reruns of movies and television remind me to be careful of everything I put in there, because I have to sit through it again on the way out.

Day Nine

Brain activity slows from swarming bees to thickening honey impossible to wade through. Thighs solidify again into concrete slabs. The pelvic nerves spread out again, this time peeling all the way up the spinal cord to the brain. The nervous system again lights up like Christmas tree as the skull elongates a foot before bursting into an electrical fire.

I am meditating in my room over lunch having no appetite. The shoulder blades again become heavy at the edges, with a vague ominous presence. This time featherless disfigured wings of a creepy mythical gargoyle emerge. Eons of good and evil mythology are played out by the subconscious. This unnerving goblin rattles about for hours before shrinking back to scraggly but anatomically correct nubbins.

Metta Day Ten

Inexplicable peace and comfort inspire the gratitude to sincerely partake in the guided loving-kindness meditation. My genuine hope is that meditating itself radiates this labour of love to as many as possible, however that works. Nothing is off the table after this modern miracle. If my identity proves to be a passing wave, a drop in the ocean, then everyone wins.

April 19th, 2004

I was still pouting on the ride home from being torn away from my calling. Attempts to talk too loud or too fast were stifled by gut aches and painful hand spasms. Apparently, the body does not appreciate being shaken out of a deep trance either. I took the hint to shut up while breathing through cramps and contemplating what this all means about life.

April 20th, 2004

Meditating at home was stronger after each course. Each week was new and different inspiring commitment and intrigue. Conscious equanimity toward subtle sensations remained strong unless it was sabotaged by my need to prove something to someone about the essence of health. Objectivity with daily life circumstance was harder to come by.

I recreated the Vipassana lifestyle as much as possible to feel as good as possible. The meditative relief itself did not translate directly to the real-life stress relief. I had lost the alcohol abstinence as an aftershock from course one. Overeating was a worse hinderance to meditation, but both should recede on their own accord.

The teaching never failed to prove itself right. You cannot target physical healing any more than spot reduction with weight loss. Symptoms depend on how deep the roots go plus the myriad of environmental factors—social, physical, and emotional. Ever-humbling is the principle of awareness balanced with equanimity. In spite of complaining, I appreciated Goenka's singular insistence on purification above countless details, health side effects, and final goals.

The simple genius of the technique allows gradual adaptation to the new energy frequencies and mental realities. The chances of happiness are increased with every step up in consciousness. Feeling better at each level allowed for embracing the journey over the destination.

That reminded me of a Ken Wilber article entitled, *"Can You Be Enlightened and Still Be an Asshole?"* Stories of fallen gurus made no sense to me then, having assumed that liberation includes some kind of social intelligence. The disgraced spiritual teachers who abuse money, power, and sex, proved that the meaning of enlightenment can get lost in translation. The Goenka version focused on the letting go of egregious flaws that prevent any shenanigans. In that case, the impulse for sexual abuse or financial fraud subsides long before the first stages of freedom.

Enlightenment was still inconceivable, but baby steps in equanimity was a good place to be. A slow deliberate path illuminated levels of consciousness as progressive inner development. Less defensive, offensive, and contentious meant more peaceful, mindful, and tolerant. Maturity, generosity, and civility sounded like purpose, love, and responsibility. I could live with that. Trauma, like vice, was not as hardwired as generally thought. The human condition was reframed within this saintlier potential.

April 29th, 2004

The physical nature of Vipassana pointed to the origins of yoga poses. Gravity and muscle tension at every conceivable angle revealed the buried sensations. Focused awareness and breath releases subconscious restrictions. Holding the pose liberates the tissue of electrical debris. Yogis can maintain the asana while awakened all night. Without soft tissue resistance the perfected poses are displayed as a spiritual endeavor.

A yoga mindset at the gym elevated workouts beyond physical fitness. Being present with the tension induces the peace and euphoria first that trigger endorphins or cannaboids later as the runner's high. The release of sensations frees the potential of metabolic enhancements from stretching and strengthening. Mindfulness will maximize the biochemical effects of any activity.

Awareness enhances all therapy just as distraction interferes. Equanimity during massage, acupuncture, and chiropractic improves symptoms more than the physical treatment alone. The physical reality obscures the true influence of the subject. Traditional medicines that originated in the minds of mystics require the inner responsibility of the patient.

Belief, meaning, and expectations impact suffering of physical symptoms. Without stress-induced spasm, a back feels better no matter the injury or diagnosis. In spite of multiple factors, the subjectivity of the person was revealed as the central foundation of healing.

I appreciated the power of observation itself. The ever-present witness endures over passing thoughts and emotions. Finally, the dramatic details in meditation can be accepted as meaningless and impersonal in the context of a non-changing onlooker. All the elaborate antics are distracting stories to purge.

The true nature of awareness escapes us in everyday life. Beneath all the noise is the silent power of purpose, love, responsibility, and freedom. The simple beauty of this *one thing* heals everything. Meanwhile the essential insights of *change, suffering,* and *no-self* still escape me.

6

ROMANCING THE STONE

June 9th, 2004
Outside Fresno, California
Fifth Course
Eight-Day Satipatthana

The thought of returning home was a bit depressing but a new outlook and support system made everything more hopeful. I found a month-long review course in ophthalmology that, not coincidentally, was two hours away from a California Vipassana center. With my future retreat schedule uncertain, I signed up for a consecutive serve and sit before the college-level intensive.

I flipped through *Power vs Force* by David Hawkins, MD, at the airport bookstore. Yet another psychiatrist with his take on the mind, body, and spirit. Judging the book by the cover blurb, I had read enough of that stuff. Without second thoughts, I walked out.

Day One

Anapana is only revisited at the courses and it is fascinating to see how it changes. I am grateful for the magnetic field embracing the head that holds the focus on the breath. I am humbled and happy to admit the improvement is not due to sheer force of will. Worries of work however still dominate for attention.

Day Two

The physical absorption of the breath persists alongside hours of droning anxiety. A heavy fatigue causes micro-moments of sleep with a slow-motion fall into my lap. The recurring loss of consciousness forces an uncomfortable head bobbing reminding me why I hate naps. Upon righting myself, the blue white brightness strobes under the eyelids, hinting of the nature of consciousness as a literal inner light.

Vipassana Day Four

The Vipassana Day sign on the bulletin board comes with a grateful smile. The forgiving surge of sensations with the first dip into the field of Insight blows past any arrogance and laziness by taking up precisely where it left off.

Day Six

By day six the spinal cord is aflame, tormented by dozens of razor blades. A fifty-pound backpack of knives slice up the shoulder blades for hours, proving that it's not over until it's over. In the distance, a friendly voice that describes **purification as a refinement of the personality** *grabs my attention to bring much needed solace. Yes!*

Suddenly, the ground shook as a thirty-foot dragon turned back on its hind legs, staring me down in high definition from ten feet away. There was no time for the bright green scales and burnt fishy smell to prepare me for the fire snorting, acrid smoke, and threatening yellow eyes. This virtual reality was more shocking than the psychedelic dreams of the sixties.

Day Seven

Grandiose plans are abruptly interrupted by a magnetic lockdown, holding me bolt upright. As the brain erupts into a few feet of flames, a swath of spinal nerves billows six inches behind me, while the pelvic nerves whip up like jump ropes. Astonishingly, my quick-dry shirt flaps in the electrical breeze. Scanning the body is like wading through honey littered with thorns. That is a pleasure before razor blades slash through my back for hours on end. Layers of barbed wire eventually slide off the front of me like a sweater, leaving a raw torso as vulnerable as a burn victim.

Day Eight

Morning starts with fine silk shirts that mutate into electrified cashmere before repeatedly peeling off in layers. Each time, the entire spinal column is cut down at the sacrum, falling forward like a giant redwood right through the chest. The pelvis is left smoldering before the tailbone swoops around the body like that dragon's tail. Seriously?

That was just a prelude to what is happening in a chair after lunch. Bare toes violently scratch at the carpet as the corners of my mouth turn up in an unnatural snarl as if possessed by a werewolf. It scares me to tears wondering what the hell is inside of me.

Metta Day Ten

Metta day brings unearthly peace beyond measure. Relief of the cold-blooded past comes with a heartfelt compassion toward all living creatures. The desire to share this good fortune with all beings overflows during Metta meditation. For all my black stones, I have no doubt that self-purification is the best I can do to help anyone else.

On the rideshare back to Palo Alto, I recalled a few spiritual teachers who wrote about having surgery without anesthetic. Interestingly, they all endured root canals using their own meditative prowess. A deep enough state could position awareness far enough from the body to observe with equanimity. The severity of sensations was likely diminished over decades of training.

I shared my new theories of pain with the captive audience. Subtle sensations in meditation must be of the same basic nature as the gross feelings in everyday life. Just as in Vipassana, the level perception determines the quality and quantity of experience.

First, you can intentionally go deep a la Vipassana to dig up the latent sensations. Second, you can live happily on the surface until the suppressed guilt eventually overflows with mental or physical symptoms. To hammer the point home, the third way is to whack your knee with a baseball bat, flooding awareness with what is already there. If the bat hits you just right, your attention is knocked out of the park for a spiritual homerun. Like random near-death trauma, it allows a glimpse of higher realms without decades of sitting still. That slim and risky possibility makes this deliberate endurance race the smarter, safer way to go. Any way you slice it, the digital programs that create all torment reside within consciousness. Crickets.

July 27th, 2004

After a month of classroom meditation, I checked the California Vipassana schedule at an internet café to squeeze in one last miracle to hopefully highjack my future. I applied for the opening a week later.

Checking email while scanning sensations, the absorption makes it hard to keep my eyes open. Breathing up and down, the translucent spinal column lumbers to the edge of its moorings. Like the sequoias before, the vertebrae fall as a unit, through my chest, smashing to smithereens on the keyboard. I glance up at a passing student as if to ask, did you see that?

August 4th, 2004
California
Sixth Course
Vipassana Day Four

Four days of soaking in sweat is not from the 100-degree heat. After three years of travel and writing, I am haunted by unrelenting doubts of returning to work—and wasting this opportunity. With minimal concentration, I seriously consider writing this one off. Even Vipassana Day is unlikely to work its magic this time around.

Breathing up and down the body, I am stunned by the compassionate vibrations that embrace me after the failed Anapana. Being forgiven for my sins by a higher power takes on new meaning.

Day Six

With eyes top of mind, I probe inside the globes to detail the cornea, the lens, and the retina. The mystery of near and far-sightedness would have to involve these informed energy fields precisely embracing the gel-filled eye like a beach ball. Additionally, ocular muscle tone also mirrors the level of consciousness by meticulously governing the shape, and thus acuity, of the eyeballs. I had a light-hearted bet with myself to finish The Meaning of Health before needing reading glasses. Looks like I can double down for another few years. Cheers.

Day Eight

Gratitude is especially prevalent this time, given the shaky start. After days of dredging the nervous system, repeated lobotomies turn the brain into oatmeal, oozing over the edges of the skull. Violent purging flattens the torso paper-thin while balancing the head still in 3D. Frigid cold fumes evaporate off the right side of the body like a block of dry ice right up to the midline. A children's choir sings eerily in the distance only when the air conditioning kicks in.

Metta Day Ten

With perfectly timed salve for the wounds, I enjoy sharing my merits wholeheartedly. Without selfish distractions, I join in the noble celebrations with greater appreciation. I promise to seriously honor the work while holding results loosely.

August 17th, 2004

Back in Vancouver I received a call from Nishe, whom I had met at the California center. Inspired enough to call at a break, she knew I would love this consciousness workshop she was attending. "Have you read David Hawkins?" That name rang a bell. Her reference was enough to pull the trigger on his trilogy at Banyon Books before the trip home.

December 29th, 2004
Kauai, HI
Seventh Course

I still cannot believe my good fortune of finding Vipassana when I did. Had I not been in Vancouver, I would not have easily heard of it. Permanent centers were just being established throughout Canada and the US, which made frequent visits convenient and accessible. Even if I found it twenty years earlier, repeated courses would not be possible with the travel involved.

I had avoided hit-and-miss spiritual trekking by having the same teaching here in the homeland. Having said that, Hawaii couldn't hurt and Winnipeg winters do. Vacations and entertainment were less interesting, but meditation was a good excuse to get away and see other centers. I stepped out of the Oahu terminal to smell the tropical Hawaiian air after midnight. The doors locked behind me, forcing me to hunker down on a concrete bench until my 5:00 a.m. connecting flight to Kauai. Awareness and equanimity always got into high gear with the travel challenges.

The cement mattress and backpack pillow required the Vipassana yogis' routine of remaining alert while asleep. Comforting sensations provided an energy sleeping bag and some protection from the traffic. That was good practice for roughing it the next day in tents on the beach, in the rain, with perpetually crashing waves. We wrapped ground sheets around a picnic gazebo for the makeshift meditation hall. Great fun.

Day Three

After a couple of days focusing on the very tip of the lip, a ballooning magnetic field engulfs my head and face to keep thoughts at bay. Like an archeologist chipping away at a sacred site, the ground below the lip literally breaks through the skin into a cavernous passage. A discrete three-inch channel washes my attention away like whitewater, circling the interior torso through the perineum, up the back, and under the skull. I recall Goenka mentioning the lip sitting on an important energy point. That was a sneaky acknowledgment of noting the subtle anatomy in a meaningful way. Aha!

Day Six

The evolutionary catharsis continued with insects, reptiles, and mythological creatures crawling out of the body as if it were a clown car. Huge forces reshaped the body into a flattened pest with transparent wings. An exoskeleton immobilized my head and encased the body. Spontaneous smiles reminded me that like posture, vision, and charisma, facial expressions reflect the confluent levels of consciousness. Empowering.

Day Seven

Since the physical structure is fading fast, I wonder if an anatomical framework of subtle energy seen in ancient texts is next to emerge. The natural breath flows easily around that inner circuit that alternates in size and consistency.

Day Eight

The channel lining the pelvis prolapses right through the perineum, spilling my energy guts. At least I hope that's what it is. Bizarrely, intestines fumble further past the cushion through the floor to flap like a dolphin's tail.

There is nowhere in the world I would rather be than sitting on a beach in Kauai on New Year's Eve. This is my perpetual resolution. The neighborhood pyrotechnics did not detract from the peaceful inner fireworks. Days of determined sitting have dissolved regret and resentment, proving again forgiveness to be a literal release. Accepting the physical truth of emotional pain allows it to dissipate. Silent awareness liberates noisy suffering, and with it, verification of the survival purpose of pain.

May 18th, 2005
Toronto, ON
Tenth Course
Vipassana Day Four

Vipassana Day came early with a stabbing pain in my right flank waking me up at 3:00 a.m. I remained half asleep until the gnawing ache shook me up for good before the 4:00 a.m. gong. Nothing would rain on my parade this solemn day, except maybe the frightening stream of bloody red urine that greeted me before lunch. Cancer flashes quickly until that piercing wake-up call reminded me that common things are common—a kidney stone was more likely.

It had been tricky teasing apart the metaphysical sensations in meditation from mundane medical symptoms. What happens on the cushion does not always remain on the cushion. Medicine and meditation are equally humbling. Enlightened monks and yogis still die of cancer. Darn.

The course manager was accommodating, offering a ride to the nearby hospital for narcotics if things got worse. But facing the impending labor pains was a defining moment that required a clear head, with a little help from my friends.

Late afternoon Vipassana rituals are accompanied by romancing the stone alternating with anticipation of screeching agony. If ultrasound could break up a stone, laser-like focus could certainly take care of business. If disease originates as a disruptive bit of information, then renewed vibrations should be able to heal it, eventually.

A dull throbbing recurs on the same lower side. Single-minded attention prepares me to face razor-sharp pain as the stone tears through the plumbing. The vague ache coalesces into a localized grain of sand which I grab with precise magnetic forceps south of the kidney. All-absorbing fields steady my hands to see it through to the end. The rocky pebble is trembling more than me as each breath nudges it a few painless millimeters down the ureter. The secured floating stone grinds to a halt in the top corner of the muscular bladder. This anticlimax must be my root canal moment.

*Having dodged a bullet for now I contemplate next steps. Then I remember that it is **passing the stone** that hurts more than childbirth. Opps! **Dhamma will support you** has never been more welcome.*

I had proclaimed Vipassana a miracle cure, the secret of life, and the fountain of youth. Living life was another thing. Right effort was a paradoxical surrendering of a desired goal. I liked Hawkins' explanation of a *yang* determination in the commitment but a *yin* attitude in meditation. Hurry up and wait.

Ananda was Buddha's cousin and loyal assistant. He had trained thousands to become enlightened but was too busy himself to attain beyond the first stage of Sotapana. After Buddha's death, Ananda was tasked to become fully liberated within days in order to join a conference of five hundred enlightened monks transcribing all of Buddha's teachings. Desperate and straining, Ananda had forgotten his own advice, repeating "I must become an Arahant, I must become an Arahant." After a few exhausting nights without progress, he lamented, "I am not an Arahant, I am not an Arahant," whereupon the divine light opened up as his head hit the pillow.

Any time desperation arose I heard the refrain to *be like Ananda, be like Ananda* by accepting the truth, forgiving mistakes, and trusting the technique. My loving presence and charming persona had not reached the stage whereby anyone noticed. Eating mindlessly and drinking alcohol were still works in progress. Negativities and judgments remained. The genius of purification meant that each year was a glorious baby step forward. The journey was the thing.

September 2005

I remained in denial about the kidney stone, hoping it crumbled and passed without notice. Four months later, it took the concentrating power of Vipassana Day of the next course for the pesky concretion to declare itself still stuck in that upper valve of the bladder. After breakfast, forcing my will on the irritant only served to ignite the whole plumbing system into violent spasms.

Retching in pain beyond the reach of mere observation, I caught a ride to the hospital. Stay out of the organs!

Dry heaves in the waiting room, I quickly recovered with a shot of smooth muscle relaxer the doctor had phoned in. By the time he showed up, the x-ray was clear but for his diagnosis of constipation. Aha, the x-ray proved the paralyzing effect Anapana had on the gut. But I highly doubted irregularity had instigated the worst pain of my life.

He knew I was a doc from the nearby meditation center. He knew one of their doctors was a Vipassana teacher. Perhaps my desperation, unshaven face, and grey hoodie explains why he refused me a prescription to get through the remainder of the course. They were muscle relaxers, not opioids! His ego could not let go of the constipation thing. Power trip.

The good news was that I finished the course without any emergencies. The bad news is that I did not go to the urologist. That was until months later as meditation deepened at home. The torso ballooned like the Michelin Man before squeezing down to Pencil Man. That meant crushing down on my old trapped stone like a pebble in a shoe. I shocked the surgeon by knowing the stone's size and location prior to the CT scan, just out of sight of the abdominal x-ray. Equanimity was not strong enough to overcome peeing razor blades for a week after being ripped apart by the scope.

February 2006

After ten courses my desire and tolerance for alcohol was fading fast. The social habit was stronger than the physical craving. I could not imagine myself as the Perrier guy. This belief made it hard to admit if a couple of light beers had any effect on my meditation progress. But I was fascinated by the reverse alcohol tolerance and the implications for all vices. The consensus was that an alcohol habit required the constant vigilance of lifelong abstinence, as it could come roaring back with one sip.

Meditation grew stronger each week and sometimes each day. Always new, always teasing. That alone inspired devotion. The daily lifestyle was ever-more enjoyable. Looking behind the curtain of reality was a rare gift. Despite the sluggish changes in life, the sheer power of awe-inspiring experiences was enough to conquer any doubt. Repeat episodes of dried blood, childhood cramps, and static electricity that lit up the bedroom when I threw off the covers brought smiles to my face.

Mindful fitness was helpful in sustaining daily awareness. Exercise was a way to feel the gross body simultaneous with the subtle bodies. The muscles tense against gravity as attention breathes right through limbs. Awareness through the full range of motion increased efficiency. Equanimity allowed a few more burning reps while preventing injury and disease. With expanding purpose there were endless ways to play and enjoy.

No doubt that aging was often accelerated with the buildup of electrical resistance from a lifetime of emotional reactions and environmental interactions. No wonder hardening beliefs and ingrained routines brings more crankiness than wisdom with age. Maybe meat needed tenderizing because of the stress inflicted on animals from factory farms.

Apropos of nothing, an irregular boulder protruded through the full thickness of my right quad. Half the flexion was abruptly blocked and held by a magnetic field for over a year. This proved my pulled muscle theory as any sudden move would tear the muscle in half. Goenka did not mention anything about subtle sensations bleeding into everyday life.

May 16ᵗʰ, 2007
Toronto, ON
Thirteenth Course

Day Three

I never thought of fatigue as a sensation until it started to recede during Anapana. I only fell halfway into my lap before head-bobbing awake. The four-day grogginess that plagued me from day one was lessening. Eight days of breathing meditation is now a possible maybe.

Day Five

All experience is happening within this field of sensations with its own anatomy and blockages. The inflating and flattening of torso and limbs make it clear that the insentient body just sits there while the whole sensorium lives in a concurrent energy field. We are not our bodies!

The shape-shifting manifestations suggest that daily experience takes place in the same subjective field. I only know my body indirectly through sensations that create the physical impressions. I see intellectually how my whole sense of self is tricked into identifying with appearances while missing its ethereal essence. I just cannot quite get over it yet.

Day Seven

The body slowly balloons into a giant beach ball before deflating completely into a windswept sail. The pencil-thin limbs are a footnote as the spinnaker doubles up on itself, spiraling into a flawless oval. My body is precisely twisted and fashioned into the inner turbines of a conch shell with bulbous frog eyeballs protruding from the thin outer wall. Blink.

The geometric precision exposes the invisible templates that guide biological variation throughout evolution. In junior high, I missed exactly how the golden ratio and Fibonacci series reflect the mathematics in nature. Without arms or legs, I settle in for hours, contemplating the intelligent designs in every minute crevasse.

When the Buddha says ignorance is the cause of our suffering, he does not mean we are stupid. He means we are unaware of the deeper source of our discomfort. When he mentions purification, he does not mean we are impure or sinful. He means we can release the biological programming that underlies unnecessary stress. The truth of what we are is clouded by the not-so-subtle electrical storms of our evolutionary inheritance. Vipassana is a somatic exercise to clear the physical remnants of mental debris.

June 10th, 2007

In the meditation hall, the etiquette for stretching legs demanded pointing them away from the teachers out of respect. It became more than politeness when impurities began pouring out through the toes. Not infrequently after intense burning sessions, red pinpoints remained on the tips of the toes, matching the exit points of the acupuncture meridians.

Years before Vipassana, after watching a nonstop action movie I was unable to bear weight on my right foot. From nothing, it felt like I broke a toe. Gout had occurred to me, but the pain settled down over a couple days and never returned. I had noted normal uric acid levels during my recent kidney stone workup. Good enough.

Vipassana heals the body without us necessarily knowing which emotion plugged up which organ system. The mind feels better without needing to know all of the neurotic details. Alternatively, in therapy, reasons for mental health issues may become clear without necessarily feeling better about them.

July 15th, 2007

I got interested in vegetarian food during an Ayurvedic medicine course at the Maharishi University in Fairfield, Iowa, 1995. Animal flesh lost its status as food for me at the Indian buffet. Meat was redundant when nutritious, well-prepared food was the best tasting and most satisfying ever. Initially for health reasons, a vegan lifestyle gradually conceded to the health and wellbeing of animals and the planet.

The simple vegetarian food offered at Vipassana courses is aligned with the non-violent precepts. The practice included taking on the role of humble monk or nun. The modern concerns with pesticides, over-processing, and impure dairy did not exist in Buddha's time, or even forty years ago when Goenka began. I had no problems with accepting whatever was served until reading Gabriel Cousens, MD.

My two most inspiring mentors came down on opposite sides of the nutritional debate. Both medical doctors who strayed from convention, both psychiatrists advanced in consciousness. Cousens' *Spiritual Nutrition* championed a live food, "veganic" diet as the most supportive for meditation. Heavy on supplements, his program of pure water, air, and sunlight won me over. He would prescribe meat to students to slow down spiritual energies that got out of control.

David Hawkins was a lifesaver for the explaining consciousness without emphasizing any particular tradition. His words resonated with my experience more than anyone else's. He laughed telling the story of his health-nut doctor friends who avoided additives, toxins, and processing by brown-bagging it to medical conferences—and of course, they were all dead. The power of awareness could overcome the bad vibes in the environment without living in a bubble. I leaned heavily on that advice to avoid some of the neurosis that plagues the holistic health community.

Vipassana was my security blanket when the purest food, air, and water were unavailable, unaffordable, or impractical.

November 5ᵗʰ, 2007

Mindful awareness appeared in every new therapy that I came across. Novel cognitive behavioural therapy, integral coaching, and aversion therapy all relied on trusting relationships, mutual beliefs in the process, and a safe environment to examine the fear. Confronting the pain in a controlled situation without reacting, resisting, or retreating sounded a lot like Vipassana. One thing healed everything. And that one thing was observing reality as it is, calmly and objectively.

February 14ᵗʰ, 2008

I had tired of reading the VRI books. The same examples and words did not help digest my black stones. I had to put the blind spots on hold to avoid twisting my brain into knots. I got the hint that the intellect alone will never see through the layered teaching. I finally accepted that the insights of *change*, *suffering*, and *no-self* were only known within the silent experience of meditation. My old assumptions had me on the lookout for profound words of wisdom. I had to give myself a break and give it a rest.

I even got tired of journaling. I learned the hard lesson: my personal precious details are useless distractions. For all my health theories, my life was not going anywhere fast. I would cut the cord when I saw it.

June 6ᵗʰ, 2008

More than a few teachers had noted from my intake form that I was still drinking. They asked about my plans for long courses that required two years of abstinence. Serious students seemed to graduate to twenty days as soon as they qualified with a handful of courses. Eight days of Anapana was still insurmountable for me. Or maybe it just gave me an excuse to drink.

I was not going to quit booze temporarily just to get into a course. When I give it up, it will be for good. It was only a matter of time as two beers felt like six and interfered with evening awareness. One sip of wine went right to my toes. Then on June 6th, 2008, I got a call at work from a teacher.

I had signed up earlier than usual for a September course near Toronto. This eight-day advanced course required no drinking from the time of registration. Usually on the honor system, this live-in senior manager runs a tight ship. She gave me the option of committing to abstinence for the long hot summer or postponing the course to enjoy the festive libations. No judgement.

Gulp. I swallowed hard as frosty mugs and outdoor patios flashed before my eyes. This was another defining moment. I was not going to humiliate myself by valuing booze over Vipassana. The body was already over it. In the suspended silence, I knew this was the accountability I needed to take the plunge. I told her I was done.

February 21st, 2010

Dad died.

From an early age, I knew dad was a little different. Different from other dads. Different than me. I saw good intentions in his glass half-full views. But he struggled to say anything positive. We enjoyed watching comedy and I learned to make him laugh just to share something and affirm that someone was in there.

I asked him what he would do if he won the lottery as he had no real hobbies or bucket list. His impressive vegetable garden was more of a money-saving venture than a passion. His maddening responses were limited to sarcastic catchphrases and one-liners from old movies. I began to accept this curiosity yet needed to figure out what made him tick. What did he want out of life, why did he have me, and how do I avoid becoming like this?

My friends and I enjoyed listening to motivational speakers, particularly their catch phrases. "What you resist will persist," was a Zig Ziglar line that hit a chord with us. I knew I had to accept the odd traits and understand the frustrating ones in order to have a healthier relationship with Dad without turning into him.

His gradual slide into memory loss was my opportunity to glimpse his basic humanity. He laughed when I kidded him that dementia had no perceivable effect on his personality or his lifestyle. We sat at the same picture widow he had stared through for fifty years, making fun of the neighbors. It was the same distant silence that Dad used to stare through his cornflakes at breakfast, as if I didn't exist. He never wanted for anything and never complained. Maybe the lesson was to accept life as it is.

Now dependent on family, it was shocking to hear Dad repeatedly express appreciation for dinners and cleanup. It took unavoidable embarrassment to force him to communicate. It was heartwarming to see this softer side. I meditated beside him during his last few weeks in hospital, with failure to thrive. I brushed his teeth and gave him a shave. "Where am I?" "Why, what have I got?" "Let's go home." If equanimity is the yardstick, maybe he was some kind of cranky old Buddha. He died like a peaceful yogi, leaving me pondering his lifelong demeanor.

Needing something to say at the funeral I finally discovered my answer. Peace and quiet! That was all he ever he wanted. Every Saturday afternoon: "I'm going to take a nap." "Can you boys keep it down?" That was what we shared: peace and quiet.

He avoided risk for it. I risked everything for it. He suppressed stress for it. I studied it. He napped; I meditated. He liked his routine; I liked my routine. His was a forced silence that shut out the world; I wanted a silence inclusive of others. His anti-social behavior pushed me toward a civilized way to arrive at the same place. Proud to carry on the family tradition, I dedicated this book to our mutual life purpose.

7

Truth, Beauty and Goodness

January 4th, 2013

I always wanted to know what fellow meditators were experiencing. Goenka advised not to compare with others to save us from envy, or resentment, or something. He did not mention the subsequent guilt from occasionally spilling the beans. I couldn't tell if the blank stares I got from my black stone stories were because I missed the whole point or because of the taboo about talking. I learned the hard way that even longtime meditators were all over the map and asking for specifics was a meaningless faux pas. Ten years later, I had no idea if anyone else went through the same Anapana agony that had dashed any hopes for taking a long course.

It was nice to see the same lifers at the various meditation centers over the years. Most serious students graduated to the longer courses as soon as they had the prerequisites. Students and teachers had urged me to get on board as no significant progress was expected from introductory courses. Apparently, Anapana was heavenly bliss for them. Once I became aware of the hidden sensations, there was no way to stop them from intruding on the tranquility promised with four days of concentration meditation.

Kindergarten courses were still challenging enough to keep my hands full. I used this great patience to balance my desperation for mind-body healing. Teachers had confirmed my suspicion that the number of long courses said nothing about equanimity or spiritual attainments. Personal destiny was written in the same information fields that determined one's attraction and commitment to the path. Letting go of my Vipassana résumé, I would dance with the truth that brung me.

All the benefits of the purified mind were conditioned on letting go of any desires to attain them. Like healing back pain, the highest levels of emotional freedom and peace were side effects of staying focused on the task at hand.

This same composure needed for healing applied equally to writing about the healing effects of Vipassana. My personal and professional passions had to be toned down for any real progress, at least while meditating. I was slow to piece it together that like loving-kindness and morality, health is just an intention until purification makes it so. The rising gratitude and certainty brought trust and willingness to persevere.

April 19th, 2013

The first feeble considerations of handling more days of Anapana came over the last few courses. Gone was the unrelenting fatigue, head pressure, and grinding back-stabs. I wouldn't say blissful, but I broke through the intolerable forces that made one more day out of the question. Then an opening in my schedule inspired a search of upcoming twenty-day courses. Career frustration was eased by the increasing chances of glimpsing a deeper truth about wellness. I took the confluence of events as a sign to take things to the next level. I was ready.

July 12th, 2013
Shelburne Falls, Massachusetts
First Twenty-Day Course

I spent the weekend on a tall ship knocking about Boston harbor. While searching for hotels, ads for sailboat accommodations reminded me of the last time my life took a fortuitous bounce on the water. Plus, it was cheaper.

Being at any Vipassana center was like coming home and Dhamma Dhara added luxury living. There was always a kinship with meditators, but the twenty-day people brought another level of community. We made it. And finally, a new evening discourse to anticipate. I wondered what Goenka could say that he hasn't already said.

Day Six

The first five days pass with little regret or critique of my every life choice. Sailing through Anapana in relative calm assures me that the time is ripe. I reframe my eagerness for the real work of Insight as not being attached to bliss and tranquility of the breath. My anticipation is stifled by the lack of the usual V-Day signage. Wishful thinking finally gives way to the fact that I miscalculated one third of twenty. Ugghh! Another two days of this.

Over the course of the morning I get my attitude in check, for the most part. But the speed bump shakes up the guilt of somehow abusing, exploiting, or monetizing my beloved Vipassana. Worse was the perennial fear of doing something wrong, spinning my wheels for years in the wrong direction. I yield to comforting advice that continuity is the secret of success for aligning errors and ignorance. Perfection only comes at the very end of the journey. Two steps back. Get over yourself.

I never nap at home or at a course. But with the extra time, reclining seems like a good way to pace myself after a lunchtime walkabout. The magnetic field about the head gently holds thoughts in check as a prelude to the future of sleep and prevents the grogginess of napping. Gazing right through my feet hanging over the edge of the bed brings back an image of evaporating dry ice that only confuses my understanding of change. Change does not seem to work with vaporizing impurities, so I substitute Goenka's synonyms impermanence, ephemeral, essenceless. Not bad.

Subatomic particles do not pass away but rather flash in and out of the quantum vacuum, maintaining the bodily structure. We are here to witness a universal truth, but ingrained mental habits only pass away by those doing Vipassana! Still so much unlearning to do.

Day Fifteen

Equanimity is good enough to ignore my intellectual roadblocks to enjoy hours of watching the ethereal paint dry. Energy streams endlessly from the body with little drama. Resting comfortably during routine surveillance, a line from the evening discourse trips up a decade of defensiveness. **Understanding annica is more important for equanimity than the depth of concentration.** *Wait, What??? How is anything more equanimous than silence?*

Understanding the changing nature of subtle sensations provides the power of purification. *My bloody black stone rears its ugly head once again with a vengeance to bite me in the ass. Accepting sensations as subconscious healing gave me all the equanimity I needed. Watching the smoldering embers of my past releases all the impurities I can handle in spite of my whining. I have to admit that in a technique that needs the mind to get past the mind, specific thoughts probably matter—ya think? My longstanding assumption that deeper is better sent me into an emotional tailspin.*

*A flurry of doubt floods my body for hours with waves of guilt and despair. Had I misread the teaching—**the sharper the focus during Anapana, the stronger the purification in Vipassana**? Body and* *mind swirl in the endless torment of a decade of contentious resistance. How many years have I squandered? How demented to miss what is obvious to everyone else? I had faithfully put my black stone aside trusting it to pass on its own accord along with other dimwitted ideas. I twist in the wind for days before a glimmer of light shines at the end of the tunnel. A forgiving silence takes the reigns to weather the storm. That very same stillness seems to purify the mind and body. Ugghh!*

Yes, life experience and positive psychology had taught me early on that everything comes and goes. I have easily surrendered possessions and circumstances of no lasting value. But the argument to stop identifying with fleeting sensations is confusing. I am still not sure exactly how my sense of self comes from these illusory sensations. Identification with passing thoughts and feelings is not done on purpose. My gratitude comes from the practice doing the job for me in spite of me. Only a higher power can extricate me from this existential attachment disorder.

Day Nineteen

A fledgling equanimity was par for the course from day one. Motivation came more from the release of subconscious tensions than by my murky understanding of arising and passing. Admittedly, future healing is more in focus than however these sensations are behaving right now. I look past present sensations to their underlying patterns that beg for release. Curiously, it feels like co-opting the present moment to face the past in hopes of a better tomorrow. The technique is very forgiving by giving me more than enough work. This all adds up to wrestling with reality as it is in spite of dragging my feet in analytical quicksand.

It had to be semantics and over-thinking that kept the Buddha's primary insights of Insight Meditation out of reach. It took ten years just to realize that these insights are not literal bullet points. The wisdom in wisdom meditation is not just profound philosophy. The three characteristics of experiential reality, anicca (change), dukkha (suffering), and anatta (no-self), are the keys to the Buddha's unique realization. Sensations always change, suffering is in resisting the change, while the personal self is an illusion of the change. If you know one, you know them all. I am zero for three.

The Buddha taught that Vipassana was **the one and only way to full liberation**. The various Buddhist traditions tweak the translations and priorities of the same noble path, yet each remain strict about *the one and only way*. Their definitions and experience of enlightenment must also be different. The beautiful Buddhist books barely mentioned subtle sensations or purification. No wonder the consensus of western teachers is that meditation cannot uproot the subconscious shadows. Besides years of meditation, they recommend many more hours of sitting in therapy, counselling, or coaching to dig up the deepest neurotic roots.

There had be a wrong way if teachers kept hammering on the right type of awareness and understanding. It seemed that Goenka was targeting the majority of people from other traditions with different types of training. Being sold on sensations from day one, the endless drilling down on equanimity with sensations made me second guess my every move.

I was more than happy to sit with the pain no matter what. I could not imagine wasting this opportunity to play games with sensations given all the pleasure-seeking opportunities back in everyday life. But **continually increasing the understanding of change** remained unclear. Listening to the same introductory discourses for ten years likely did me no favors.

Teasing apart these differences made me even more grateful for Vipassana "in the tradition of S.N. Goenka", which for him meant his teacher, "in the tradition U Ba Khin". Cute.

The physical challenge of purification suited my disposition toward practical healing. I was happier to pursue slow but steady wellbeing than seeking inconceivable states of consciousness that may never arrive. Buddha's version of liberation came second to purification rather than prioritizing the bliss states that may miss some of the tendencies to be an asshole.

Metta Day Twenty

I realize the brilliance of the breath as the preferred mechanism for Anapana in preparation for Vipassana. The forced touch of the breath settles to a barely perceptible thread of respiration. Then, with only awareness itself passing over the lip, the subtle sensations offer a glimpse of the energy fields wafting throughout the whole body. The absorbing lip ties down the mind just as the magnetic body parts absorb thought during Vipassana. Awareness is always awareness no matter the activity. Modern mindfulness training for temporary stress relief misses the permanent release of deconditioning the mind. Ah-ha!

My black stone is beginning to crack. I accept my decade long mind freeze enough to let it just sit there. I trust the technique itself to eventually clarify blind spots, notwithstanding inevitable detours and distractions. The power of the daily experience gives me the humility to embrace any long-term ignorance. I know my heart is in the right place—the same place that attracted Vipassana to me in the first place and vice versa. I am happy to surrender my personal willfulness to the higher power that is doing the purification.

I am thankful that all the previous years of ballooning and shrinking, morphing and crushing, created the opening for a good week of constant release of subconscious particles without all the drama. Of course, that respite is quickly challenged by a thumb-sized spike digging into the left lower flank reminding me there are always more layers to unpack. Stripped away from reactive muscle spasm the precise gnawing residue just glows mysteriously from its source.

I see how energetic blockages lead to future disease. Then symptoms create the stress reactions that double back to multiply the strength of the original buried emotions. Heightened awareness digs up the seedlings long before they grow into illness. The level of consciousness determines the perception of pain confusing the self-diagnosis and the possible need for medical intervention. The genetic, environmental, and lifestyle interactions feed back into the confluent information programs in consciousness at the essence of ailments.

November 5th, 2013

Very slow resistance training became the yoga of weight training. Half of the weight and one third of the speed allowed mindful endurance during a prolonged burn. Gross and subtle sensations with detached awareness meant body, mind, and spirit were all represented at the gym. The muscle tension squeegees the energy blockages into awareness. Uncovering new aches and pains previewed the challenges to look forward to at the retreats.

I always nursed a few glitches around joints that hindered full range of motion or strength. These are the vague symptoms that medicine ignores and chiros love getting their hands on. A stubborn right hip and deep aches below the knees were always confounding. It made no medical sense that a few lunges thirty years ago were the source of intermittent kneecap pain all this time.

Holding a military press brought out the tension in the deep neck muscles reminiscent of that ballooning throat chakra. It had been a decade since the same knot dropped me to the ground, almost losing consciousness. Reading at a picknick table, the side of my chin was precariously perched on my palm. The weight of my head suddenly gave way to a rifle shot that felt like a dislocated facet joint. Of course, x-rays were normal, but my chiropractor was banned from going anywhere near it for ten years. Now the weight training revealed there was more work to be done.

August 15th, 2014
Toronto, ON
Second Twenty-Day Course

Twenty-day courses became the new normal, with a couple of short courses sprinkled in between. There was no turning back now. I had been motivated by mental suffering to seek truth and healing. But the gravitational pull to the future now equaled the push from the existential angst of the past. With a real possibility of genuine peace, the need to fix everything was less critical. The clear direction itself eased the insistence that life keep pace with the drama on the cushion.

The registration form asked about life changes that had been noticed since starting Vipassana. My past enthusiasm of mental and physical improvements now felt overstated. The most dramatic change was the contemplative lifestyle and the ability to meditate itself. No one raved about my radiant personality. The sports clinic would go out of business with this timeline for healing back pain. A life coach would be fired with the failure to convert sitting into action. But permanently deleting an alcohol habit was evidence enough of psychological and physiological change. It was hard to stay excited about something that was not there anymore.

Day Four

The theme of this second twenty-day course is the new level of stillness. Not the psychological peace from a hike in the woods but inner quieting of the mind and the senses. At times the magnetic suction drowns out thoughts entirely, or at least the attention to them. The choice remains to stay with the absorbing force or follow some trivial ramblings. It is an up-close look at how the self-sabotaging ego tries to survive in spite of a golden chance to evolve. The personality would rather be right than step into the unknown promise of the silent self.

By bedtime a gentle cocoon of silence is more restful than sleep. Alternate wakefulness and lucid dreaming leave me surprisingly refreshed. **When the world sleeps, the Vipassana yogi remains awake.**

There is none of the usual fatigue. For years, I could barely keep my eyes open for the evening schedule and fell right into bed. I was too tired to consider fatigue as a sensation until it went away. The added vitality makes extra minutes of sitting more valuable than resting or walking. A quiet mind makes the body less stressed. Like many feedback loops in the body, the stress-free physiology adds to the mental harmony.

The opposite is also true. A noisy mind stresses the body. Then anxious thoughts reemerge from the same fears encoded in bodily tension. In every course, after days of purging, thinking becomes more positive and benign. Each time we burn off another layer of negativities, the return to life enjoys a diminished stock of pessimism. Refinement of the personality means living in the daily optimism of a less reactive mind and body. Thank God.

Day Seven

Inner silence is synonymous with the acceptance, forgiveness, and surrender that psychology and spiritual teachings ask of us. The physicality of emotions offers a literal way to let go of resentment, regret, or resistance. More than just saying it, taking responsibility is like actually dropping a weight, hanging from the rafters, or enduring sixty feet of water pressure. It has nothing to do with engaging or requiring anything from others. By facing the inner electrical reality, we discharge the secret pleasure of victimhood and blame.

The same mental silence triggers the parasympathetic source of endorphins and cannaboids of peace while toning down the sympathetic source of cortisol and adrenalin during stress. The less reactive mind is more tolerant, patient, and understanding. Unconditional love and peace are the default qualities of equanimous awareness.

Day Ten

Secure in the knowing *was the expression that popped into my head as the perfect answer to a life of resistance. My whole life, I wanted to know something certain. Education in science and medicine required regurgitating secondhand knowledge. I could not promise or peddle what I did not experience for myself. Even reading about the four noble truths is not that exciting. Experiencing a deepening truth meant my desire to be* **beyond reproach** *was more than a perfectionist's excuse for doing nothing.*

The instructions **to become established in the technique** *flooded my consciousness with new meaning. It is poetic justice that a long-sought career that is second nature only comes from knowing my primary nature. Impersonal sensations are ironically the most intimate experience possible. Gratitude and humility arise because this cleansing power is not of my doing. If I could have purified myself, I would have done it years ago.*

I do not need meditation to correct all my shortcomings anymore. I do not have to prove myself right by ranting on the limits of medicine and psychology. I do not need to prove consciousness as the source of all healing and illness. I do not have to cure all my injuries, prevent all disease and defy aging before declaring this journey a success. I do not need to convince family and friends that I am not an idiot who wasted his life. My purpose is secure in the knowing. Inner health and happiness include the imperfections of outer appearances.

I finally relent—subtle sensations are meaningless minutia. I concede the whole sense of self is somehow cobbled together via stories created from subconscious feelings. I had never before grasped the drastic idea of dying for a cause. But when the cause is the very purpose of life, I willingly sacrifice myself for the greater good without losing anything.

Day Eighteen

Yes, long courses are necessary for the black stones and hidden rock formations to start crumbling. Obvious from the perspective of abstinence, alcohol interferes with conscious development. In retrospect, the stock of sensations as the inborn karmic load highjacks our opinions, worldview, and free will. Personal responsibility for animal instincts and collective ignorance heeds the Buddha's warnings of the dark forces of Mara. The devil made me do it.

Blind spots of arising and passing are inherent in the same blinding sensations. Misreading the insights comes from too much thinking and not enough doing. Ditto with the moral precepts, the noble truths, and the rest of the teaching. Understanding means directly knowing for yourself. Just do it.

I now delight in the chanting of annica as a celebration of the unique feature of this tradition of Vipassana—the subtle sensations that get you in the purification ballgame. I knew it all along. Whoohoo!

The occasional silence opens the mind to the non-changing subjectivity of who and what we really are. Identifying with this elusive awareness is the goal of all spiritual traditions. But only diligent dissections of physical irritants release recalcitrant trauma and addictions.

The mental contents are seen as passing illusions in the foreground of a never-ending silence. Suffering is identifying with thoughts and sensations, whereas peace is yielding to the persistent background of pure subjectivity. The inherited pain/pleasure wiring is gradually unplugged. The human condition is supplanted by unconditional awareness.

Reading a dozen Vipassana Research Institute books did not offer much more perspective than the evening lectures. I needed new words and new metaphors to shake off the long-standing brain blocks. The writings did give me an appreciation of the difficulty in translating the 2500-year-old teaching.

In all the contention, I forgot that atoms and molecules are just condensations of charge in magnetic fields. It was reasonable that the nervous system sensed information from an enveloping energy field like a radio receiver. It was easier to see sensations as the body's translation of ethereal information into awareness rather than the tinkling of subatomic particles. Then perfectly organized, meaningless, chaos made more sense.

There is no greater pleasure than the end of desire.
—Daily Words of the Buddha

The Buddha loved lists. There are the five friends and the five enemies, the ten virtues, the eight factors of enlightenment, the eightfold noble path, the four noble truths, and many more. Memorizing was never my thing. The best I could do is get the gist of a list from patterns and meaning. There was nothing like silence to capture each point in one memorable snapshot.

The virtues, the factors, and the friends are inherent loving qualities. Both the means and the ends. The hindrances and the defilements are the habitual fearful traits. Unconditional silence is healthy and conditional emotions are toxic. Nothing to memorize.

The degree that one enjoys truth, beauty, and goodness in life reveals the level of inner peace and lovingness. The optimism in the eyes of the beholder makes the teaching sound less pessimistic. Life is only miserable in the context of an imperfect expression of absolute perfection. An expanded context of change would blow a hole through my black stone.

8

THE MEANING OF HEALTH

January 2014

One of the Buddha's lists that spoke to me was the Triple Gem. *I seek refuge in Dhamma, Buddha, and Sangha* was part of the Vipassana Day ritual of surrendering to the power of nature, the qualities of the Buddha, and the collective vibrations of meditators past. These aspirational motivations were more inspiring than the steady stream of *life is suffering, everything is changing, don't identify with it.* I had to look up the word refuge to resonate with the safe haven that the teaching was offering. Stop the world, I want to get off. I understood the truth that *Dhamma will support you* by doing the heavy lifting of purification. If only I could get out of the way.

Some version of truth, beauty, and goodness was revealed by many ancient and modern philosophies. Ken Wilber clarified and unified all interpretations of It, I and Us as the knowledge spheres of Science, Art, and Values. His Integral Theory showed that these consistent inner truths manifest as Society, Consciousness and Culture. ***Dhamma, Buddha, and Sangha***. I had refashioned it to Purpose, Love, Freedom, and Responsibility in writing The Meaning of Health.

March 13th, 2014

If not lazy, I was attracted to working smart rather than hard. Knowing consciousness as the way to a wellbeing, I had long stopped expecting conventional medicine to shine a light on genuine healing. Vipassana had confirmed where the light was for steady, progressive wellness. The one thing that points to the essence of everything meant that, like the fountain of youth and the secret of life, the bullet proof soul was really a thing.

Medicine cannot wrap its head around a subjectivity that is more than mere emotions and opinion. Even mind-body science is stuck in the brain-body doorway between soothing peptides and frayed nerves. Silent awareness reveals a way of intimate knowing that is beyond both reason and feelings. Pure awareness is actually more objective than the linear facts and statistics that are only as useful as their context and meaning.

Holistic, functional, and integrative medicine honors this inner life of the patient. Intuitive docs and newer technologies reveal that changes in consciousness influence genetic, hormonal, and biochemical expression. The trust and belief that underlie the placebo and nocebo phenomenon are being valued beyond getting drugs to market and scaring the public. New non-drug therapies for addictions, traumas, and neurosis facilitate a safe environment for the patient to face symptoms directly until they diminish. Bearing down on pain or pleasure without reacting heals at any level of development to some degree or another. The habit patterns within consciousness are vulnerable to mindful attention. One thing.

June 21st, 2014
6:00 a.m.

The Essence of Psychology
Oh, this is my mind

These swarming energy fields contain the conscious, subconscious and unconscious mind. Three-dimensional frequencies encode for animal instincts, cultural paradigms, and personal habits. This electromagnetic cloud of repressed pain and emotion is broadcast like radio programs. The brain and nervous system tune into the stations like an antenna to attract resonating thoughts and emotions that repeatedly harden into a familiar way of being.

This interior state becomes my outer state via a feedback loop of reacting to a partial view of the environmental threats. This vibrating reservoir of suppressed trauma and fear secretly creates the worldview that undermines hopes and dreams. Moods, attitudes, and values are sourced from this same cumulative influence of upbringing, education, and life experience.

This ephemeral aura literally hijacks the nervous system to create sensations that filter reality on the way in and again on the way out. It colors the view of myself only to be projected onto everything and everyone else based on how they make me feel. People and circumstance can only trigger what emotional weapons are already there. Those patterns cast blame or take responsibility for internal suffering that only appears to come from outside.

Cumulative fears and desires block or inflame precise hormones and peptides that reinforce mental states. People with similar levels of consciousness resonate with mine, in the same way that particular music, food, and entertainment are preferred. This electronic smokescreen begs my attention if I want any semblance of free will.

My very identity becomes one with an all-encompassing but partial field of felt experience. The full potential of my personality and mental wellbeing is stifled by this magnetic fog. But for the mercy of this subconscious lockdown I can no longer deny the living hell just below the surface.

Oh, this is my level of consciousness

Levels of consciousness are literally levels of awareness and equanimity. The strength and endurance of emotional reactivity reflect where we are on the stairway from fear to love. The degrees of being offended, defensive, and contentious mirror our vulnerability on the sliding scale of identity. We can only see out from the level where we are standing.

Vipassana intimates that all conscious growth comes through observing mental contents whether meditating or not. Dr. Robert Kegan's Subject/Object Theory shows how child development happens naturally as the subject stops identifying with mental objects at one level to become the subject of the next level.

Loving discipline facilitates a child to endure the misery of a tantrum until it passes, in order to discover more acceptable behavior. Traumatizing and haphazard at best, child development is at the mercy of the modelling of family and culture. As adults, the cultural norms and laws are low bars for the higher reaches of human nature. The self-help movement promotes the personal responsibility to face adult tantrums that missed the loving discipline the first time around. By intentionally observing the objects in consciousness they lessen their hold on our inner sense of self.

The resilience, compassion, meaning, and independence vital to happiness are impacted only so much with lifestyle, therapy, and coaching. These therapeutic modalities hope to improve function at the current level of consciousness. It is impossible to uncover the myriad of causes of why we are miserable and will not necessarily make us feel any better. Whereas Vipassana feels better without necessarily knowing why. Higher consciousness defends against the social and economic pressures that hinder wellbeing. The chances of happiness at any level increase with a more conscious relationship with life.

Contents of the mind are sustained by the same electromagnetic fields as the material body. No wonder the communication between cells and between people is not fully explained by the nervous, immune, and endocrine system. The collective social and cultural influences on mind and body are feedback loops within the same electromagnetic fields.

True healing deletes the negative programing in the subconscious software. When the clouds are removed, an innate regenerative nature emerges no matter the specific sorrow that inspired the Buddha. The necessary hardships can be faced without making things worse by with the unnecessary suffering of denial or blame.

The Essence of Health
Oh, this is my body

I am sitting in the mind, the body embraced by a knowing field of energy. The whole field dissipates into a greater non-material field of consciousness. I only know the body and the field indirectly by sensations felt by the mind and observed from a higher awareness. Pure subjectivity is obscured by the sensations and emotions that grab my attention.

The same fluctuations contain both the thought fields co-mingling with matter fields to create an obedient biological structure and function. All life is psychosomatic in that the subconscious encodes the instructions for metabolism, immunity and repair. Any physiological imbalance and injury proneness are due to limited information getting through the mental filters.

Moment to moment stress adds to the electrical interference in the material fields to divert the full vitality of the life force. Positive attitudes and healthy lifestyle are only as good as the strength of the innate healing presence that would limit symptom severity and enable treatment response. Only this flow of consciousness can reconcile inexplicable medical mysteries, spontaneous healing, placeboes and noceboes. Marathon runners drop dead and hardened prisoners die of old age because of the myriad complexity written in unique karmic fields.

The stress-relaxation response set in consciousness informs the autonomic nervous system to recreate that level of awareness in the biology. Modulating the metabolism, the word goes out for the precise balance of cortisol and endorphins to govern the physiological pillars and moment-to-moment attention. The physiology manages the pollutants, chemicals, and manmade frequencies in the context of purpose, love, responsibility, and freedom, to determine the final level of resilience.

The buck doesn't stop with the brain and the genes. The brain is not sentient itself but relays the specific frequencies in and out of consciousness where memory and learning take place. The evolutionary habits carved into the genome are not necessarily destiny. Genetic expression and neuroplasticity are in constant flux with the collective emotions, behavior, and the environment.

The objective study of this subjectivity is the original research of the Buddha and the final frontier of medicine. The ultimate person-centered therapy facilitates the patient's power of awareness and attention. The healthiest lifestyle is this perpetual inner growth to prevent, heal or cope with whatever comes along. Until deconditioned, the human condition is trapped in a revolving door with its animal instincts on one side and its angelic potential on the other.

The Essence of Spirituality
Oh, this is spiritual reality

A spiritual path is the waking up to one's true nature, cleaning up impurities, and showing up in deeper relationship with everything else. Buddha taught that Vipassana is a scientific exploration of mind-body reality as it is directly experienced, not as it appears to the senses. We start where we are, proceed at our own pace, and trust to the extent we know for ourselves. We are left to our own devices to navigate the terrain with basic instructions. He's a character.

Silence confirms a familiar truth beyond time, space, and medicine. Complete ancient healing systems are direct insights not discovered by tinkering around in a lab. Even great scientific insights come from intuitive geniuses. Language cannot translate the transcendent experience very well. Only ignorance could distort and misuse the wisdom of both mystics and scientists. In the meantime, I let assumptions, beliefs, and expectations run through my fingers.

There is no way to know who or what awareness might feel like, a cappella—without accompaniment of mind or body. But without desire or fear the subject is free and complete. The gradual path acclimatizes the nervous system to handle the higher frequencies. This should prevent the injury, death, and madness of the mystics in the historical record that looked at the sun unprepared. A kinder, gentler deprograming engenders trust as senses and thinking stall out. Nice to know.

After Vipassana, a few minutes of Metta allows the use of imagination, visualization, and verbalization to cultivate loving-kindness. I was still wrestling with the literal effects of sending good vibes. I did not feel for myself the supportive frequencies from fellow meditators, the conducive grounds of the center, or the charged atmosphere on the cushion at home. I did not know directly the radiant care from teachers or the power from the distant community. I did enjoy without understanding how Metta serves as a salve for the wounds after a challenging course. But given my earnest hopes for family during meditation itself, an extra ten minutes to share my merits were harder to come by.

The gratitude and generosity on day ten were gladly paid forward if only in thoughts and prayers. I was completely on board with the sentiments and intentions of embracing all beings. Faith grew at every turn as the teaching kept proving itself. I would go back to square one in a second if a loved one could be partially freed. But even the Buddha could not carry you on his back. **No one can walk the path for you.**

Living through the hidden determinants of human behavior brings deep understanding and compassion. Touching the essence of suffering, it is easy to see people as more than their symptoms. Back at work, I practiced listening without reacting, to inspire without advising, by sharing what I know as a unifying presence.

September 2014

I had stopped daily journaling after five years as shapeshifting body parts were losing their charm without the life changes to match. Routine *draining the swamp* of random impurities was not as noteworthy anymore. Those first two hundred pages had swollen to many hundreds before I got the hint that I am spinning my wheels.

There was no way to decide where to end the story. Just as all progress is up to the karmic forces, a satisfying conclusion would present itself when the timing was right. A good clue was waiting out the long slow weakening of my attachments to results and the sluggish breakdown of my black stone.

This upcoming eight day immersion would be my tenth Satipatthanna course. We were allowed to read and follow along with the hard copy during the evening discourse. I had long given up deciphering the ancient minutia. But this time with less rocks in my head, I brought a renewed attitude and steadfast determination. I was going to diligently follow along in the text, the rest of my black stone be damned.

September 2014
Merritt, BC
Satipatthana
Day Seven

Wherever there is life there is sensation. This was the line that spoke to me from day one. Information in consciousness interacts with biology to churn out sensations that stimulate the behavior and biochemistry needed for survival. Every waking perception is compared to the past to produce the quality and quantity of pain or pleasure. The creature survives through instinctive feelings to friend or foe. Countless stimuli of fight or flight, repulsion or lust, multiply the fitness for survival of every last move. This feedback mechanism in the earliest life forms to remember, learn, and evolve is recorded in nested energy fields of the descendent organisms.

The same subconscious loop of perception, recognition, sensation, and reaction now controls thought and behavior in humans. But with sentience, physical feelings offer an opportunity to free oneself from mindless instincts and childhood sticking points. While the subconscious conditioning was necessary for life to evolve, we have the capacity to wake up and take it from here.

Day Eight

*The simple wagon wheel icon for this tradition never quite registered before. The wheel of suffering is finally seen as the ancient treadmill that multiplies human misery. Awareness and equanimity act to slow and reverse the hamster wheel to unwind the conditioning, now as a wheel of liberation. I was slow to put two and two together as to why a western stagecoach wheel was the symbol for this great Eastern technology. The wheel is always turning or **changing** for better or worse.*

*Just accessing the subtle sensations is the first vital step. **Annica, annica**. Yes, we are finally here in the field of insight, thank God. Equanimity with sensations is required for the right type of purification. Mental complexes take decades to resolve even when specifically allowing for them. That is why absorption alone in other traditions will miss purification. Change still does not roll off the tongue.*

My obsession with past conditioning and future healing blinded my understanding of the changing nature of present sensations. Yet, the technique is a game of percentages and part of the mind must have been doing something right. With the judging mind subsiding, the need to know all the details is lessening.

I was loving the gym now for totally different reasons. The awareness of gross muscular tension within the ghostly tingling offered new insight into exercise science. From the runner's high to the anti-depressant effects, intentionally facing pain and discomfort allows the metabolic and hormonal effects to flourish greater than with mindless movement alone. Even muscle and bone building are liberated because of the purification in consciousness. One thing makes everything better.

Gravity and body weight wring out the muscle to bring the subconscious tension into awareness. Then mindful training allows endurance for those few extra reps that create the conditions for growth. Attention itself allows more muscle fibers per contraction for a more efficient use of the time. Breathing through the muscle belly serves to unleash bits of debris for relaxation and calorie burn for the rest of the day.

9

Pinhole Enlightenment

April 2015

Vipassana had ruined vacations for me. I would be happy spending most of the day in the hotel coffee shop reading in a mesmerizing cocoon. Hedonism, beaches, and bars were long gone. There was no need for relaxing getaways, sightseeing, or adventure anymore. A guilty pleasure was squeezing in an extra dose of Vipassana anytime there was an opening in my schedule. My family's collective eye roll was palpable when informed of my being on a wait list just six weeks after the last retreat. I could take my chances booking a flight on short notice before being accepted. It was fun leaving plans up to karma and the Dallas Center registrar. Dhamma was doing the driving.

April 22nd

Sitting cross-legged, the backs of my heels begin rumbling before bulging out backward toward the groin. The calves balloon to fill the triangular space in a half lotus position. Then scanning the body in bed before sleep, the elongating soles join the calves stretching up knowingly toward the perineum. Bilateral buds form off the heels to penetrate the base of the pelvis before burrowing into the abdomen and stiffening into twin steel rods. This triggers a whole-body paralysis ten times the tingling of when my leg falls asleep. Before losing consciousness booking the flight is a no brainer, no matter the wait list or the family.

May 4th, 2016
Dallas, Texas
Day Eight

Form fitting yoga blocks spray-fill the inner torso at each chakra level leaving a central opening. The two steel rods recur now, sharpened like Samurai swords rising out of the pelvis below. Ascending with each breath the pristine blades are guided through the small openings of six irregular cuboids. **Keep your neck and your back straight!** *Fine edges facing out, the piercing tips scratch up against the inner skull lining. The detailed spiritual anatomy is spewing impurities in every direction. Fascinating.*

Day Nine

Over forty-eight hours the long metal foils meld together in the central channel from crown to tail. The foam cube at the throat thins horizontally like a pizza while five other levels flatten vertically like a spinnaker. The sailing metaphor is apt as the Dhammic breeze powers the journey for some time. As the throat saucer spins swiftly, the edges fly open like a space station satellite. This Hubble telescope, precariously welded to the cartilaginous larynx, hangs me out to dry in the solar winds for the remainder of the course.

Metta Day Ten

There is no end to my good fortune—finding Vipassana just as centers were popping up all over North America, having the time and means to travel to sites, and the wherewithal for this challenging extreme sport.

Gratitude and humility are beyond personal will in the presence of a divine power. The mind cannot heal itself. The personality cannot walk away from its own sense of self. The ego will not participate in its own demise. This requires something higher, stronger, and deeper to do the heavy lifting. Without much career ambition, I pray that an altruistic opportunity falls in my lap. I dream of an honorable cause I could get behind whole heartedly.

Then it hits me. This is my miracle job. Vipassana in the tradition of S.N. Goenka is integrity incarnate. A rare gift not to be squandered, Insight is a responsibility to share with those not ready, willing, or able. This is my long-sought raison d'etre.

With my black stone turning to sand there was even new promise for Metta meditation. Goenka assured us that everything was silently understood through direct inner experience. I accepted the notion of collective consciousness but did not literally feel the connection with all beings. These good vibrations should eventually bounce back.

If the personal self was slowly disappearing, who else to benefit from Metta than everyone else. Guided loving-kindness set the moral tone for the grace of benevolent frequencies when and if they arise. Unconditional love would have to wait in line with moral perfection and pure awareness. If there was a remote possibility of contributing to the rising tide of consciousness, I was happy to work from home.

July 2016
Toronto, ON
First Thirty-Day Course

Two twenty-day courses had gotten me over the Anapana hump. Any remaining concerns of ten days in concentration were balanced by the eagerness for a full twenty days of purification. Like a long slow run, I settled in for the long haul one hour at a time. A teacher I had met in California came to sit the course with a yoga mat in his backpack. That gave me confidence that my focus could withstand ten minutes of mindful stretching and resistance training before meals. I fashioned a discreet exercise program to partially mitigate against muscle wasting of thirty days.

Day Five

The attachment to purification shows itself with a slight hesitancy to give up observing sensations for ten days of Anapana. But the extra time on the lip breathes new life into understanding the nature of concentration. The bottomless pit of absorption eases my desperation to get on with the good stuff. A heartening whole-body envelope confirms that purification is always ongoing.

Day Twenty-Two

*Nesting energy bodies dominate the days with wide open floodgates of subconscious effluence. With one week to go, my ears perk up through the silence for the first new instruction in over ten years. **After you have a free flow of sensations, put your attention on the solar plexus every once in a while**. This one simple statement came with delight and surprise.*

This tiny acknowledgment of subtle anatomy relieved a decade of self-doubt. This tradition saw the meditative maps and milestones of other teachings as unnecessary distractions. Only the upper lip and the crown of the head were vaguely mentioned as sitting on important power lines. Admitting any meaning of this central hara point eased the guilty pleasure I took in anatomical landmarks. The leeway to choose your own way based on the types of sensations that arise had allowed some free reign. Layers of victimhood washed away with greater assurance in my own instincts.

Meanwhile, this new master switch ignites a bombshell of unchartered depths. It is reminiscent of the upper lip turbo-boosting the meridians and the pulsating blood exploding attention through every organ. This is the same pressure point that had sucked the breath out of me as a kid after being sucker punched by my brother.

Day Twenty-Eight

A gorgeous green canopy in ninety-degree heat looks and feels like Thailand. Relaxing blankly outside on a large rock, the central passages align and intensify throughout six energy levels. Radiations from the central channel pour out of the crown and the base, up and around to enclose the torsos from top to bottom, perpendicular to the horizontal illustrations of chakras. With that image, the hara plexus penetrates right through the abdomen and out the back of the spine. The openings radiate around the sides, crisscrossing the vertical lifesaver to bubble-wrap the body. Breathing through gyroscopic donuts completely absorbs any stray thoughts.

Metta Day Thirty

The communal spirit of guided lovingkindness feels like a celebration of our mutual conquests. There is only good will and understanding for all the dark forces after accepting and forgiving my own. The new layers of morality are perfectly timed. The shades of killing, stealing, lying, intoxication, and sexual misconduct are not unexpected. Don't indulge the compulsions, don't encourage others, and don't take pleasure in the vices of others. I knew that bringing the wine for dinner, cheering on cinematic vengeance, and dating quasi-divorced people would need readjusting. I had to rethink my kombucha buzz.

Noble silence ends with two welcome shock absorber days, yet the fireworks will not let me sleep. Nudged to sit up in bed, my neck balloons up with square edges enclosing my head and shoulders. Four live wires precipitate outside the spine and down the right lower limb, wrapping tightly around the foot. I am used to new incisions slicing open just as it's time to leave. Dissecting the pulsating spinal nerves as they alter in width and rigidity will add an interesting dimension to the flight home.

After lunch, I was chatting with that teacher with the yoga mat. Out of the blue, he spouts off that no one of our generation in this tradition will ever reach even the first steps of liberation. *Whoa! WTF.* I respected the commitment of the assistant teachers, but that revealed something about his level of insight. Well, I wanted to know what others were experiencing.

August 1st, 2016

It occurred to me that my black stone and the other two insights are all negative—*impermanence, suffering, and the illusory self.* This half-empty glass did not resonate as well as the opposite—*eternal, peaceful, pure awareness*—glass half-full. A higher self of infinite loving truth was more inspiring than an unstable, unsatisfying, mistaken identity. Admittedly, the technique insists on facing the pain of the downside in order to reap the benefits of the upside. Years of seeking the truth of healing no doubt contributed to a decade of wrestling with truth of suffering.

September 4th, 2016

The Vipassana lifestyle promised that life would be always evolving, not merely repetitive. Staying young at heart required the kind of continual growth normally reserved for childhood.

Bucket lists and retirement plans were redundant on a joyride that never stops giving. A constant change of scenery was unnecessary when an expanding worldview guaranteed perpetual novelty.

Merritt, BC
Special Ten Day
December 2016

I hadn't noticed the infrequent special ten-day course on the schedules until I needed one. This course offered the quieter atmosphere of a long course designed for qualified old students who could not find twenty or thirty days. I was attracted to the fresh evening discourses and losing the hourly instructions of the intro course. For over ten years, Goenka's reassuring voice, open questions and answers, and typical newbie commotion were welcome distractions from my own incessant blather. With deepening quiet, I'd had enough of the relentless racket. But like with the longer courses, it was a long day alone until joining the group sit before the evening talk.

Day Six

No surprise that eating and talking remain the most difficult times to sustain awareness of subtle sensations. That is why lunch on day six is so shocking. In the midst of slow careful bites, a cone of silence commandeers all sense experience. I need the calories, yet hunger disappears along with body weight and the will to move. I never yearned for a benevolent presence to take over daily activities. But if this is a taste of the future, I'm all in.

Day Eight

There is always another layer of stillness as sensations ebb. No impulse to think adds a quieting effect on the senses. The initial goal was to feel sensation on consecutive parts of the body surface. Next was a passing awareness of interior events. Goenka kept moving the goal posts as simultaneous sensations inside and out had moved them again. Now a three-dimensional magnetic field creates a three-dimensional silence at every point in space for a new normal.

The mind cannot be stopped by force of will. Any standstill results from the vaporizing sensations. Yet there is no end to the ego's willingness to deny and ignore when it comes to proving some point, solving some problem, or enjoying some food. The mind does not want to be silenced at its own expense. That clarifies the self-sabotage in all our efforts at self-improvement.

Metta Day Ten

In moments of silence, the altered sense of time makes hours fly by in minutes. The quieting of each point of the body distorts the sense of space. The head and the feet strangely occupy the same space defeating the purpose of scanning the body. The relative nature of time and space hints at the next domino to fall that is cause and effect. Like arising and passing, cause and effect are sufferable features of existence, suspended in a moment of absorbing silence.

Transcending misery promises unconditional love and peace—not based on the condition of external causes. It makes no logical sense that an impersonal field of information would be loving. But without reacting, pure presence would be without judgement. In one basic move, faceless silence is the ideal of forgiveness, surrender, and acceptance for which couples' therapy can only hope.

Pinhole Enlightenment

Ken Wilber had clarified the clichéd notion that we are always already enlightened. Apropos of which an inspiring metaphor came out of the blue to reconcile my detoured medical career. I couldn't help sharing it on the rideshare to the airport.

Pinhole glasses sold on late-night infomercials are based on a kernel of truth. Viewing through a tiny hole does improve vision without glasses by blocking out the myopic blur. Normally, the curved shape of the cornea deflects light rays from focusing clearly on the retina. Yet the flat central portion allows a few light rays through a pinhole straight through to the central macula surprising the patient with a cramped 20/20. While impractical for driving, the insight reveals that indeed part of us is always already seeing perfect.

In Vipassana, the pinhole is found at each point in space opening into the ever-present light of pure awareness. Each timeless ray of truth is blurred by the astigmatic errors of bodymind filters. With the courage to peer into the blinding light, a clearer Self-image appears. Pretty good deal.

Without a distracted field of vision, the familiar clarity has been there all along. The eye of consciousness provides the silent background we use to recognize sounds, the empty backdrop we rely on to distinguish forms, and the brightness we trust to see clearly. Always already. Ophthalmology never could fully explain the mystery of human perception. Changing sensations are more easily recognized in the context of this persistent acuity. Annica, annica. Change is still not the first thing that comes to mind.

January 2017

My struggle with Metta meditation is ending in a truce. Loving all beings unconditionally will take some time. But trusting that our same ultimate nature as always already there, Metta turns into rejoicing the common essence of all beings. This precise visualization of a spiritual athlete feels more righteous than wishful thinking.

> *May I be free of anger, hatred, ill will, and animosity.*
> *May I generate only love, compassion,*
> *goodwill, and sympathetic joy.*
> *May all beings be happy and free of suffering.*

January 20th

I missed much of the news and aftermath of September 11, 2001, sailing the Great Barrier Reef. In recent years, weak explanations of history pushed me down the rabbit hole of twin tower conspiracies on YouTube. I was saved from the bottomless pit of energy weapons on social media by a timely safety net. Nassim Haramein, a self-taught physicist, spent his college years immersed in nature, imagining the mathematical patterns of life. Skiing and climbing in Whistler, BC, he intuited a unifying theory of physics with only the algebra and geometry he saw all around.

He recognized that the Flower of Life carved into diverse ancient monuments mirrored the designs he was deciphering. As a three-dimensional whirlpool, he calculated that the flower bloomed into a double-torus shaped engine that sustains all of life. As a quantum black hole, this fundamental vortex generates the constant creation and turnover of everything from atoms to supernovas. Uniting the relative physics of the very big with the quantum physics of the very small came from a simple notion: the big stuff had to be made of the small stuff. Even I got the math.

This essence of matter displays a fractal geometry as a repeating spinning dynamic at every scale. Its holographic character shows that everything is always already connected via wormholes outside of spacetime. As energy donuts all the way up, they coalesce as the pattern for human chakra anatomy. As torus grids all the way down, they churn up the quantum foam of material creation perpetually arising and passing.

Direct knowledge of this ubiquitous all-knowing power awaits the deepest experience of pure consciousness. May as well unify science and spirituality while we're at it.

February 12ᵗʰ

I remain confused since the hara point sprung into life at the end of the thirty-day course. Drawings of chakras show six funnels emerging front to back at each level and a vertical one from crown to base. The solar plexus is tucked up below the rib cage, splitting the space between the third and the fifth chakra. Slouching on a boulder had thrown off my sense of this forgotten anatomy. I realize now that the hara point stays on the surface. It was the third chakra below that had inadvertently tunneled through the abdomen, revealing its conical shape. Breathing over the body in bed, I knew the other five openings must be operating just out of sight.

Without much thought, I roll over and inhale right thru all six chakra passages simultaneously. Textbook. Six narrowing conduits impale me strongly, bisecting the vertical crown passage. With only a vague recollection, the breath easily finds the landmarks that stir up new intensities and matching donut-like radiations.

I was walking a fine line of Goenka's warning about not looking for particular sensations. But just as gross anatomy guided my early dissections, I could not unsee drawings of meridians, chakras, and energy bodies. In spite of the new attractions, I always yield back to the basic instructions of equally tagging each point of the body objectively.

April 4ᵗʰ

Five days of breathing through midline holes gives coffee-shop reading the power of a formal sit, making it hard to keep my eyes open. Haramein would say it is quantum gravity that is pulling the mind to silence at every point in space. Pure awareness could be the long-sought *free energy* that powers purification.

May 2nd

The teaching never ceases to prove itself. All of the shocking details are meaningless as each point in space becomes its own spiraling chakra, equally absorbing and purging. Being strung up by trillions of push pins is preferable to one giant knife to the throat. Paradoxically, the deeper the rapture the less compulsion to explain all the concepts. But I try.

July 4th, 2017
Toronto, ON
Second Thirty Day Course

Thirteen years being aware of subtle sensations meant that ten days of concentration would not offer the blissful ignorance of other traditions. Any serenity would be superimposed on incessant oscillations. But there was no more hesitation to forgo Vipassana for the deep dive into Anapana as the two were not much different anymore.

For years, upper lip sensations were a mini-Vipassana masterclass with localized morphing, absorbing, and dissolution. Since the longer courses, progressive depth at the breath fired up the whole body. The effortless thread of the breath cycled from the crown to the base and back to cinch up the body like a sack of flour. The magnetic ties to the lip, the hara, and the chakras coerced me into submission of working smart.

Day Three

Surrendering everything on one level meant nothing to lose and everything to gain on another. It is no sacrifice to give up the lesser for the greater, the superficial for the genuine. With fear receding there is nowhere to stand and nothing to hold onto. That is until the last title of the health trilogy jumps out of the ether to prove the boy has a long way to go. The Peaceful Truth—perfect!

Day Five

The discourse reminds us that the deeper levels of absorptive jhanas are not necessary for Insight practice. Cracking open the door to work with subtle sensations requires a minimal access level of concentration. Any release of subconscious tension is enough to unlock the power of the tranquil fields as needed for the right type of concentration. Fortunately, my interest in wellbeing aligns better with long-term purification than momentary serenity.

Day Seven

The recurring white brilliance teases my peripheral vision, implying a literal light at the end of the tunnel. The blinding sunlight in near-death experiences suggests that pinhole enlightenment may be a real thing.

Vipassana Day Ten

The sacredness of the Vipassana rituals is more honored and respected as gratitude and faith in the teaching increases. The intimacy and communion are treasured like a once-in-a-lifetime occasion. The appreciation is inedible for the historic survival and transmission of this uniquely pure teaching.

Day Thirteen

My foot landed on the floor with an excruciating reminder. Over the years, various toe joints swelled and throbbed more than a shoe could accommodate. The big toe uniquely encases a tiny sesamoid bone in its flexor tendon for leverage. While pseudo-gout is possible given the kidney stone, the vice grip of the meridian running right through this mini-kneecap complicates the diagnosis. My insight to *purify now rather than medicate later* brought a trusting smile to my face.

Day Fourteen

I never know if the sleeping volcanoes that Goenka promises after the early experiences of complete dissolution are still yet to come. Subconscious icebergs are top of mind as a vague threatening presence inhabits most of my chest. By afternoon, muscle aches about the head and neck are familiar of fever. In the evening, my head weighs a ton and I cannot rotate my neck past ten degrees. Taking an Advil is a rare consideration.

Day Fifteen

An infection never comes but the neck stiffness worsens. The invading shadow is suffocating as it darkens the torso. Mentally preparing, I am actually searching my childhood for some forgotten trauma.

Day Sixteen

The gut and the appetite have completely shut down and drastic food management is in order to maintain calories for the work. I usually avoid most of the cooked entrees for the side dishes and salad fixins. But now I'm practically drinking the salad dressing for the highest calories with the least bulk. The empty carbs of white flour, pasta, and rice reinforce the slim pickins.

Day Eighteen

Yoga poses and body-weight resistance serve their purpose ten minutes before meals, cautious of the neck. Mindful range of motion helps with sitting, while sitting in turn preserves spinal extension and flexion. Coordinating energy fields pull me into strict alignment for freer flow through the gross and subtle anatomy.

Day Nineteen

A powerful peace mocks any concern for health, writing, or livelihood. All my pissin' and moanin' is laughable.

Day Twenty

An innocent bubble pops out of the familiar pinpoint on the right side of the neck. The C-spine remains the focus of lifelong blockages. The projection radiates out like a trumpet, circling back over the body to find the opposite end of a double-sided horn blowing out the left side of the neckline. Attention passes through the Frankenstein bolts to trigger the memory of a scribbled drawing of rare "chakra wings" in Cousens' Spiritual Nutrition. His rainbow frequencies fan right and left of each front-facing chakra vortex. Each spinning black hole remained as six donut holes through the body, now a sideways bagel radiates around the body through the neck. The new energy grid sparks another level of surging power throughout the sensorium.

Day Twenty-One

I am shaken awake by a demolition crew pounding on inner foundations. That gets my attention to sit up in bed to allow now well-defined wind instruments to blow out the musical notes of purification. The tone and frequency orchestrate the varying size and shape of each chakra opening. My long suspicions of the heart being so coy are upended by a tuba-size hole blowing through my chest for a spacewalk through the giant heart opening. The quantum sucking and purging echo the Big Bang and galactic black holes.

At lunch, contemplating nature's geometric perfection brings back images of those seashell turbines. Gross anatomy faded into the background with the passing of gross sensations. Now-subtle anatomy begins to fade as subtle impurities recede. The life force remains to sustain the basic biology structure and function.

That took me back to the night I breathed through the frontal chakras hidden in plain sight. In between mini-bites, I assume the position at the six lateral chakra wings. The subsequent breath illuminates a six-piece band trumpeting sideways through each vital passage. The overlapping radiations arrange an orchestral harmony of the acoustic field. Music to my ears.

Day Twenty-Three

The new tunneling pattern boosts even the hara-point superpowers. Like holding onto a rock in whitewater rapids, the raging flood tries to wash me away. This invisible force of nature is more like the wind evidenced by its effect on swaying trees, dust and debris. Thinking of lunch, a skeleton drinking a beer at a bar is a fitting image of the passing enjoyment of food and drink.

With strict involuntary alignment, the central channel enlarges into a twelve-inch cylinder from the crown through the base of the pelvis. This has an obliterating effect of the rest of the commotion. After hours of this central Shushumna taking the reins of purification, the entire head and torso deflate to a pinpoint with arms and legs hanging awkwardly from nothing.

Day Twenty-Four

The waterfalls rage on as chakras and associated wings ebb and flow like the tide. This emboldens the upper chakras to brazenly drive everything else down to the base, leaving an Easter Island-like head in its wake. The Ant Man body with giant noggin from waist to crown dissolve and refresh repeatedly over the morning.

The commandeering presence in the chest rumbles awake to solidify as a metallic orthopedic halo screwed into the skull. A football facemask anchors firmly below into the rib cage, explaining the Sasquatch-like neck motion of the past two weeks. Tears come for the child who created this protective gear to defend himself from the cruel harsh world.

This subconscious prison is no metaphor as bicycle locks now restrict the axis of two chakra wheels. Oh, the poor chiropractor who thinks he can release the spine with his hands. Years of these disc brakes pumping the throat chakra could account for the poor communication, tentative self-expression, and detoured life purpose.

The tragic comedy becomes clear with a projected visual of a crying child live-streaming divinity, still holding onto the halves of a sandwich in each hand. Self-sabotage again exemplified in the face of scary benevolence. The malevolent ego fearing loss of control is already controlled by animal instincts and childhood fears. Fuck!

Day Twenty-Five

There is no way to conceive of the transcendent level of peace and joy—nibbana in Pali. Lofty spiritual goals are unexpected gifts when the stars align. The chances of enlightenment are enhanced with the accruing karmic merit from purifying morals and virtues. But just being free of negative emotions is good enough for a life well-lived. It's these basic instincts and neurosis that really nag at day-to-day function. Nevertheless, jumping the tracks of spacetime into an otherworldly peace train could happen at any time along the way.

Day Twenty-Six

The grace of sitting in a magnetic field blanketing all thought does wonders for gratitude and humility. It also eases the impatience that these padlocks will be sawed through anytime soon. The metallic stardust blowing out of thirteen front-and-side nebulas are reassurance enough that all is well.

By midday, another physical presence appears on both sides of my head. Within the hour, the outline of three spongy heads and replica torsos branch out on each side, squeezing into the one overburdened pelvis. By the end of the afternoon, the pelvis gives way to accommodate seven complete torsos shoulder to shoulder. The traditions speak of nested energy bodies, each with their own set of chakras. This cartoon version hinted again at maximizing surface area to access every point in space.

If indeed each body has its own chakra system, it would take some finesse to feel my way through without exhausting all time and energy. This battleship board game requires military type leadership. After some extended concentration, I ineptly breathe in and out through thirty-six front facing windpipes and the seven crowns. It takes the better part of the hour for an askew inhale to awkwardly carry sideways through six apertures of seven sandwiched bodies. Now is a good time to yield back to my old routine of breathing right through all the many structures to confirm nothing means anything. No attachment!

The thirteen black holes, times seven, swallow me up with a new order of gravity. That should light a fire for the seventy-two thousand Nadis distributing Prana to the furthest reaches of the mind-body phenomenon. Seven hara torches are certainly overkill, but it is too late to turn back now. Thank God seven times the surface area means exponentially less pain as the whole sponge hockey team is wrung out to dry.

Day Twenty-Eight

The seven figures may have signaled the end of the game for the halo and facemask, but the impurities about the throat never cease. Tensions continue to bubble up from the blue hole in the neck to repeatedly disappear and restore the newly formed framework.

A perfect glowing orb repeatedly inflates from center to slowly annihilate the entire grid like a lunar halo. It takes on the previous triangular shape before doubling over itself to hang limply on the voice box like a spent condom. Nice. Over the course of the day, the deflated balloon remains hung from the larynx within the vertical channel, times seven.

Day Twenty-Nine (Evening)

Like dog collars, the locks are seamlessly integrated around the first and fifth chakra axis of two distinct bodies. Inexplicably, a diagonal iron bar connects them, spanning five bodies. So much for each body as a fractal iteration of the next. This bizarre neurosis selectively stretches across five floors of five buildings. Increasing neck stiffness is clearly related to this deadbolt around the throat with implications for all musculoskeletal dysfunction and injury.

Metta Day Thirty

Recurrent contraction and expansion of the wormhole network amplifies the simultaneous sucking and spewing at every point. I had long learned to accept leaving a course in the middle of reconstructive surgery. Mercifully, proof of life helps to ease much of the frustration. Adventures in consciousness continue to illuminate the true nature of health and healing, while shining a light on medical mysteries and unexplained phenomena.

Back Home

If I needed a challenge to my equanimity, a delayed flight out of Toronto cancelled at midnight before flying past Winnipeg for an early-bird breakfast in the Saskatoon airport did the job. Lingering peace and quiet sustained a smile while respecting my six travel companions. Nothing unexpected from the trains, planes, and automobiles that define my thrice-annual venture.

I guess I was recruited to play center with my new offensive line clearing the path. I contemplated my responsibility to the history of the game, the opportunity to play for the fans, and what the game teaches about life. I anticipated a new normal of daily practice. Perhaps a visit to the sports clinic would confirm that my joint problems were out of their league. But for sure, the cleansing lifestyle makes anti-aging medicine redundant.

Vipassana retreats remain the greatest experience of a lifetime. I speak of this perpetual gift as enthusiastically as if it's the very first time. Just to know, just to share, all prayers are answered no matter the results.

10

THE PEACEFUL TRUTH

December 8th, 2017
Special Ten-Day Course
Vipassana Day Four

Loving everything about Vipassana Day: the anticipation, the opportunity, the ritual, the community—none of which I enjoy back in the world. The Triple Gem remains my touchstone to truth, beauty, and goodness. The qualities of Dhamma, Buddha, and Sangha, inspire my own highest virtues reflected in nature, enlightened beings, and the Vipassana community. The Triple Gem resonates as the omniscience, omnipresence, and omnipotence that sustains life.

A decade of contemplating consciousness still escapes me when listening to these interpretations of change. I keep forgetting that the Buddha's insights of changing reality are realized from a higher perspective of non-changing awareness. I accept that intractable issues back in the world are always changing but usually for the worse—the wheel of suffering. Then Vipassana is the wheel of liberation that makes things better, but the wheel is always spinning! Annica!

This illusion of physical life emerges from a fleeting confluence of energy fields. The human cannot see this reality objectively until it steps outside it subjectively. A smoke screen at each level of consciousness fashions a self-fulfilling veil of truth. Until the sun burns through the fog, concrete reality is impossible to break.

Day Five

Occasional distortions of time and space are reminders of the foreverness of infinite presence. Looks like the pinhole metaphor was predictive of the wormhole web connecting all things at the subquantum level. Deepening absorption feels as if I may be sucked through a black hole at any moment. On second thought, if pure awareness is already everywhere, then when thoughts and sensations go to zero, pure awareness is left where it always was: free and clear.

> **Oh, house builder you are seen, you will**
> **not build this house again.**
> **—Daily Words of the Buddha**

The Buddha's perceived pessimism of not wanting to be born again into suffering is deceiving. Life is expendable only in comparison to undying peace. Creatures required a mindless mechanism to evolve until thoughtful beings could dispense with the automated feedback. Without fight or flight, equanimity jumps off the survival of the fittest treadmill to delete all its programs.

Metta Day Ten

Metta Day silence is always a joy that I exploit until lunchtime gossip. Hard to let go of the ethereal peace so long in attaining. Palpable gratitude makes sending loving vibrations almost plausible. All the more likely without time and space intervening. Engaging in noble chatter remains uncomfortable. Every part of my being protests forcing air through the vocal cords.

The multitude of studies of healing prayer fail to mention the level of consciousness of individual pray-ers. Goenka refers to Metta-only Burmese traditions as not generating the same loving power as full Insight specialists. Compassionate thoughts are a welcome drop in the ocean but identifying with lovingkindness itself should go nuclear. I am looking forward to that.

The aroma of fresh airport coffee calmed the usual hesitation of facing the email backlog. Peacefully waiting for flights meant the rusted rideshares and crowded subways had not completely wiped away the equanimity of the course. Sudden delight came from an animated Haramein video with identical energy flows I was noting in real time. Anatomically correct chakras, including six "wing" formations, confirmed and refined Cousens' doodling of arching rainbows. Synchronicity much?

Reviewing my course is satisfying as seven bodies were better than one for spilling impurities without much drama. Unless you call this top-heavy presence remaining from day ten dramatic. A bearskin rug drapes over the shoulders, the heavy skull weighs on my head. Lost in space with the cartoon simulation, I lose the front part of the torso. The flanks extend forward before finally touching a couple feet in front for a SpongeBob SquarePants effect on the flight home.

December 26th

It takes a week of enduring an invisible fat suit before it dawns on me. There are six more matching rows of seven bodies inside. No agenda meant no foresight of two rows packed in behind and four wedged in front. One set of arms and legs hangs off the edges. So much for the handbook, forty-nine times the surface area stretches my observational powers. If only it were so, linear calculations promise forty-nine times the purification.

The same subtle anatomy in each body echoes the fractal patterns in nature. Forty-nine crown chakras, forty-two frontal chakras and transverse wings, calls for some synchronized multi-tasking. My neck will take the fall for seven steel bars racked across the first and fifth bodies within all seven rows. Haramein needs to update the animation.

The black/white holes at each point in the mind-body field are constantly emitting and absorbing subatomic particles putting a finer point on the insight of change. These double-donut dynamics continually circulate life-giving information in and out of the infinite vacuum of space like quantum stargates. Attachment to the optimistic purification had meant ignoring the pessimistic suffering. Non-dual awareness includes both the infinite and the finite, the positive and the negative. I knew it all along.

February 8ᵗʰ, 2018

I settle in for the long haul with a supersized energy grid. Inflated calves become burning light-sabers, piercing the perineum to snug up against the interior walls of the central channel up to the crown. Hours of lasers buzzing the inguinal canals with annoying pleasure is well worth it if decades of animal lust burn away. That triggers questions of an old inguinal hernia and if this cleanse will prevent a second. The two inner beams separate from a double-walled enclosure of that long-deflated rubber for the length of the channel. Not exactly what the textbooks show of the triple walled Shushumna.

Forty-nine hara points and lip tips really ramp up awareness out to each point in space. Conflicts between medical and meditational diagnosis continue as deep burning pain in the throat spreads over the arms and chest. The heart took a pounding in recent years, awakening me with scary palpitations that I had passed off as electrical impurities.

Now I am hoping these angina-like symptoms are better explained and resolved by Vipassana than by some future angiogram.

March 4ᵗʰ, 2018

Everyday progress sustains enthusiasm and inspiration. The ominous rumblings do not usually happen at home but embers smoulder for days after a course. Each day brings stronger, deeper, and quieter sits without all the drama of a course.

Curiously, I never considered the magnetic pushing and pulling as sensations per se. But as the metallic shrapnel recedes these attractive-repellent forces are clarified into a silent standstill. Either way, powerful absorption compels an eager surrender of the meanderings of the personal will.

March 9ᵗʰ, 2018

Radio silence changes the motivation of being pushed by the past to being pulled by the future. Dropping old ideas, emotions, and pleasures are as tangible as dropping dead weight. Lying on a bed of nails is more tolerable than being skewered through major organs. Locating identity in awareness itself lessens the personal threats that drive daily stress. No self!

March 16ᵗʰ, 2018

Both science and spirituality concur that there is no self. Medicine sees people as genes and brains. Impersonal biochemistry requires no conscious say in healing or illness. Spiritual teachings agree that beyond the ego, impersonal habits are running the show. So, the personality is either hijacked by the biology or by the subconscious. Yet some essence in consciousness must still define the person. Namaste.

*As a medical student, I could never articulate my innate bias that something within the patient was more essential for wellbeing than a medicinal fix. No wonder the intellect cannot win the argument of free will. The personal will is part of the illusion of subtle sensations. Increasing consciousness means the freer the will from subconscious programs. Eventually, freedom **from** will ensues as personal will is absorbed back into the will of Dhamma, the Divine will, or cosmic consciousness.*

March 20th, 2018

One thing heals everything. The more silence the more healing. The miracle of human awareness is that it changes objects in consciousness that are weaker than they appear. Silence is golden.

March 23rd, 2018

The centers serve basic vegetarian food aligned with the moral precepts of not killing. Renouncing the house-holder life, students accept charitable room and board without too much complaint. At home, my preferred live organic vegan food and supplements were not always available, affordable, or practical. Now with Vipassana as my swiss army knife when all else fails, I still leaned toward a holistic lifestyle to support consciousness.

Dr. Cousen's Tree of Life Center did not teach meditation but offered a pricey ten-day green juice fast with yoga, meditation, and spiritual talks. BYO Meditation only filled a few hours daily, yet there was no hunger with three daily all-you-can-drink veganic spiced greens. It was interesting to learn that detoxing comes mostly from fasting itself. Starvation mode supplemented by nutrients releases heavy metals and toxins from the fat stores actually visible in the high colonic effluent. Good to know that my low-cost low-calorie Vipassana courses supplemented by insight would suffice for a regular cleanse.

It took a week to get my gut moving again. Food influenced my dreams and my sleep enough to think it was affecting my twenty-four seven awareness of sensations. It was like my bodymind begged to be a breatharian monk. Fitness and food were ever-more enjoyable playing second fiddle to mindfulness training, but all were mutually beneficial.

June 19th, 2018

Hawkins' books remained my most supportive companions daily since 2004. I would never have felt his words so deeply without simultaneously scanning sensations and vice versa. Without referring to a particular tradition he wrote about letting go by observing vibrations, proving that the terrain was the same no matter the vehicle.

The reader was inspired by being *"already gifted"* as a committed seeker, *"already very far advanced"* being devoted to love, truth, and all of humanity, and *"destined for enlightenment"* as only one in ten million are even interested. With all my suspicion of sending and receiving Metta, I had no problem travelling to bask in the glow of the two most evolved beings I knew. Just in case, I was in on the fun as Hawkins shook everyone's hand to plant the seeds in consciousness. I hedged my bets with Cousens performing Shaktipat by touching the crown to bestow higher frequencies on his students.

September 8, 2019

The subtle subconscious blockages were not that subtle anymore. I have been limping around for months as multiple channels cut through the right hip joint. In spite of normal strength at the gym, I wondered about degenerative arthritis. But rotating waves through various muscles suggested fluctuating impurities. Meditation and medicine are both humbling games of percentages. A unifying compromise had the same universal cause expressed as imperceptible origins to full-blown disease. Equanimity looked directly into the presence of the past to increase the chances of rewriting the future.

September 18ᵗʰ, 2019
Twenty-Day Course
Montebello, QC
Day Two

Anapana is now just an aspect of Vipassana with the lip being a **part** and the breath being the **flow**. Both result in quieting the mind as sensations vaporize. Both lead to underlying habits begging for release. But some things never change. Practicing Anapana, I cannot wait for active Vipassana. And doing Vipassana, I welcome a nice spot to rest in peace.

Day Eight

There is no desire for exercise at the breaks as the breath is taking up all the oxygen in the room. Hawkins words, "The path is short, waste no time," hit home after Goenka's story of an Indian man sentenced to death—a sword to his head—if he dropped any wine crossing the festival grounds. Tolerating thoughts along with the breath is not good enough anymore under the threat of beheading. Then I vaguely heard Goenka mention the concentration requirements for the various steps of liberation. Each of the four stages of enlightenment came after a dip into a progressive level of silent absorption. Without much clarity, I took the hint to up my game.

Day Ten

The wheel of suffering is a hamster wheel of constant seeking and securing. The wheel of liberation is equanimous with eons of stress as the ionic breeze circles the drain of each chakra. Locating the self in pure subjectivity begins with feeling life streaming in from every direction. The magnetic silence is enough to leave the personal will up to the prevailing powers that be.

Day Eleven

Beyond students being attracted to Vipassana to differing degrees, there is no comparing the inborn stockpile of habits, the strength of commitment, or the recognized value. Compassion for each person comes from realizing our common condition, just showing up, and not thinking in terms of credit or blame for the progress.

The magnetic effect is as strong as the first course, but more obvious now with less ground glass and razor blades. A nervous system tuning into underlying peace then broadcasts the harmony to other beings in the same way that misery loves company. Whether we hear it, feel it or capitalize on it depends on our level of consciousness. That's the loving-kindness of Metta meditation.

The lock around the base chakra is the remnant of a decade of burning concrete that was the right hip, thigh, and knee. It explains the lower back pain and injury-prone right lower limb. Now seven energy legs squeeze into one, igniting thirty-five scorching toes. The handbrake around the throat separates out to include the third eye chakra above for three distinct deadbolts across five subtle bodies.

Day Fifteen

A Dark Night of the Soul might explain the eerie depression that hangs over the day. The gloominess finally breaks with the sudden breach of the lock around chakra five. The broken crossbar allows the ring strangling the throat to gently float over one body to the left, stopping at the central body. All three chakras are less-tightly wound now as the connecting rod hangs in tatters.

If the near dissolution of the body in year one was indeed the stage called bungha, all the senses and thoughts were still operational. Apparently, the senses shut down in the fourth level of concentration but thinking remains. The stark difference of the enlightened state is a complete silencing of thought as well as all senses with cognition itself being the last of the fleeting sensations to go. There is no way to comprehend who or what is left to be aware in pure awareness.

Day Sixteen

There are no words to describe the serenity from a purging central chakra. In the mindless delight, the loosely wrapped base lock on the left unexpectedly shuffles to the midline, aligning under the fifth like the cylinders of a bank vault. Looking ahead and behind, that robotic event multiplies by seven ghostly rows. I assume the forehead lock will follow suit at some point. This is the kind of finale that usually happens on the escapade home. Blessed.

Day Seventeen

The realization comes that I have ignored the radiations emitted out of the crown chakra that encircle the torso as an elongated donut. Lightly scanning up and down, inside and out, the three-dimensional tornado ramps up until all forty-nine explode into awareness.

Day Eighteen

The broken crossbars and overlapping emanations bring unforeseen electrical storms. Seven legs unravel like twine wrapped around lawnmower blades while the locks around the seven base chakras spin like pinwheels. Concerns of a hip replacement ease up as the glitch in my giddyap disappears overnight.

Day Nineteen

I assume many subconscious volcanos have already erupted. For all the threats over the years, these deadbolt boots on the throat, forehead, and base chakra, speak to my intractable life issues. Third eye destiny, throat self-expression, and base level back pain all limit forward progress in life. Chakra characteristics, like personality types, and medical diagnoses tend to feed into the patient's projections—until and unless purification proves the case.

October 16th, 2019
Back Home

The combination padlock around the third eye finally finds its bearings and inches centrally to align with the throat and base chakra below in the middle body of the home row. The softened lockbar bows off the forehead down the inner right torso to rest against the pelvis, multiplied by forty-nine. The locks are distinct from the chakras, without radiations or inner whirlpools. Spacetime toys with my head as each of the forty-nine bodies feel like the true self as I pass by each of them.

November 3rd

*A decade of "Daily Words of the Buddha" continues to inspire morning meditation. **You are your only refuge.** The Triple Gem is united as the teacher, student, and teaching are shown to be one vibrational truth. The tricky little aphorism of the knower, the known, and the knowing is reconciled with unison of all holy trinities. The universal teachings of a higher self, one's true nature, and cosmic consciousness are indistinct.*

The detailed lists of virtues, factors of enlightenment, and five friends required cracking some cosmic eggs. Purification puts Humpty Dumpty back together again. Equanimous awareness is the one silent truth that unifies, clarifies, and simplifies all the teachings. Unconditional love and peace are innate qualities in the fluctuations of spacememory— Haramein's term for the learning and evolving dynamic in consciousness.

The vitality of the physiology is informed by the level of consciousness or the strength of the life force that gets through at each level of ego filters. The frequencies at each level of awareness are realized as the advancing identities and worldviews from selfish to selfless. The same loving discipline that facilitates growth in toddler tantrums is used in cognitive behavioral coaching to reframe suffering for adult education. The human mind evolves naturally by being OK with pain every step of the way. Buddha exploited this natural mechanism for complete liberation of suffering.

November 20th

Walking around without sharp twinges of hip pain rules out any serious arthritic damage. Still, roving tightness indicates lower limb logjams.

I am not an Arahant. I am not even a Sotapana—the first glimpse of nibbana. I have not jumped the tracks of spacetime. I have not purified all mental blemishes. Acceptance and patience come from being on a secure and certain path. Spiritual clichés resolved, all therapies in context, all partial truths respected. The journey is the destination.

The central nervous system is a radio antenna tuning into a communal subconscious. The ethereal clouds are dispersed by the sunny disposition of equanimity. The innate loving broadcast then resonates with karmically attuned hearts. The only way to reach everyone everywhere is at the same time in the same space—a collective field of consciousness that is always already, universally present. Beyond hopes and prayers, the lovingkindness power of Metta is in practicing Vipassana itself. God bless.

February 11ᵗʰ, 2020

Time and space display the same neuroplasticity as the brain. Distinct and distant parts can strangely overlap the same space. Hours of meditation go by in a flash. Watching the rolling ebb and flow of thought and sensation is not unlike the hours staring down undulant waves off the prow of the schooner.

For all my resisting, the teaching reminds us repeatedly that understanding only comes with direct experience. The intellect cannot see beyond its own thoughts. The wisdom of impermanence comes by locating oneself in permanent peace. The Buddha can only speak about existential suffering from a perspective outside existence. Insight into the illusory self comes from the vantage point of the actual Self. Ground-level change is just not that inspiring from the ground.

Buddha was an independent thinker trusting his instincts to go up against cultural pressures. Achieving the highest levels of absorption in other traditions, he refused their enlightenment credentials. He was honest about his residual stress even after passing through the eight jhanas. It did not take him long to realize a more purified nibbana after dissolving all lingering doubts. A new type of enlightenment, free of all suffering included the roots of the shadow.

Meditation often uses mental or physical objects for concentration without concern of the experiential truth. Vipassana begins with changing reality of the breath on the body as it arises and passes. All mindful absorption is helpful, but the full stock of subconscious impurities is missed if not deliberately sought. Incidental sensations that arise in concentration provide only incidental purification without intentional equanimity.

Conventional enlightenment does not necessarily expose the deepest roots of suffering. Even here with purposeful dissection, the stock of sensations diminishes slowly over the years. Emphasizing the right type of understanding and awareness means purification is the primary goal. The right type of nibbana means that the depth of unwholesome habits has been released with innate loving discipline in the tradition of S.N. Goenka.

Knowing how the mind works at all levels brings unique insight to enhancing treatment at any level. Coaching and therapy already facilitate confronting, owning, and letting go of pain. Shadow work accepts and releases repressed emotions. Responsibility works.

Feb 12th, 2020
Merritt, BC
Special Ten-Day Course
Vipassana Day Four

Reality is an illusion that still has to be managed. In spite of constant change, life is real enough to care about, participate in, and support others. White knuckling one's security is not sustainable as things come and go ad infinitum. However rare, a stable perspective transcends and includes all the instability. Any real certainty transcends and includes all partial truths. There is nowhere to look but within.

For days, persistent nasal congestion appears without allergy, infection, or emotional upset. The broken tire iron, still hanging off the locked brow, side swipes the face, putting pressure on the sinuses. Symptoms in meditation use the same information to mimic real life experience. Only habits that are already there can be triggered by the environment, emotions, or strict observation.

Day Eight

The developing embryo faithfully follows the energy templates now seen as the seed, fruit, and flower of life. These three-dimensional vortexes at the smallest scales both power and guide the growth and development of all things at all scales. Haramein had the vision to generate the numbers of nature's innate spinning geometry.

The yin-yang and I Ching, Star of David and Kabbala Tree of Life, and the Holy Trinity and the Jesus Fish are all two-dimensional icons of the same apple-shaped engine of creation. This universal algebra unifies the fundamental nuclear, gravitational, and electromagnetic forces in nature. Prehistoric civilizations hint at gravity control by transporting thousand-ton blocks miles over hills, valleys and waterways. Ancient monuments on every continent perfectly aligned with each other and the cosmos means someone had a view from above.

I am always on the lookout for issues of the heart, given my relationship history. But those regrettable missteps hide the fact that my heart is generally in the right place. The newly exposed restrictions on intuition, communication, and basic instincts could put that to bed. Perhaps that cannonball run through the heart and a few years of midnight palpitations are lessons in love.

Speaking of which, a distinct whirlwind gathers speed in the chest before the heart vortex elongates eerily through the abdominal cavity. Like the famous Munch Scream, a sloppy heart chakra drives the three lower chakras deep into the pelvis. Times forty-nine.

March 9ᵗʰ, 2020

Keep your head and back straight, this will help you. *Aligning gross and subtle anatomy serves to unkink the ethereal garden hose for unimpeded flow of energy.*

Each pinpoint in space is now its own teeny chakra as an essential energy dynamic driving and sustaining creation. The Buddha confirms that these quantum whirlpools spew trillions of particles in a blink of an eye. All religious legends and myths are revealed as the same tortuous purification of forgiving all ignorance.

March 25th, 2020

Knowing one insight, you know them all. My black sheep of *change/annica* is finally embraced as glaringly obvious. *Suffering/dukka* is appreciated as the constant threat, annoyance and insecurity of that constant change. Pleasure is even more miserable because of the anticipation, disappointment, and loss of desired circumstances. The *illusory self/anatta* is often the last to know. But letting go of the ego's death grip on change allows the patchwork of the self to fall apart on its own accord. The three characteristics become one direct experience of inner reality. Annica!

Consciousness fills in the missing pieces forgotten by science and religion. Awareness reveals the inexplicable healing in medicine and miracles in the scriptures. A complete inner truth allows the appreciation and respect for the partial truths of all disciplines. Life still insists on sickness, tragedy, old age and death, but is now more bearable with the right type of awareness and understanding.

April 1st, 2020

Two weeks into the pandemic shutdown and not much had changed from my normal routine. I vowed to use the opportunity to finish this draft of the book. For years, I stuck to my story of waiting to see how it ends before wrapping things up. It is no coincidence that a nice story arc resolving key questions, lessons learned, and reconciling a contrary life lands during forced isolation. Everything comes in threes and the door remains open for the final piece of a trilogy. Hopefully it does not take another seventeen years for the realization of *The Peaceful Truth*—the deepest experience of a lifetime.

I was so thankful for sneaking in one last special ten-day course before all centers worldwide closed down for the foreseeable future. It was no accident that just as my current awareness could withstand an indefinite break, this would be the longest stretch between courses. My daily Metta now honestly embraces the centers, the students, and humanity in the deepest way possible.

GLOSSARY

Anapana: Respiration. Anapana-sati—awareness of respiration.

Anatta: Not self, egoless, without essence/substance. One the three basic characteristics of reality along with anicca and dukka.

Anicca: Changing, impermanence, ephemeral. One of the three basic characteristics of phenomena along with anatta and dukka.

Arahant/arahat: Liberated being, having dissolved all impurities of the mind.

Bhunga: Dissolution. An important stage when apparent solidity of the body turns to subtle vibrations.

Buddha: Enlightened person.

Dhamma: Nature; natural law; law of liberation i.e., teaching of liberated person.

Dukka: Suffering, unsatisfactoriness. One of the three basic characteristics of Nature along with anicca, anatta.

Jhana: State of mental absorption or trance. Eight levels attained by practicing samadhi (concentration), bringing bliss and tranquility without eradicating roots of mental defilements.

Kalapas: Smallest unit of matter many-fold smaller than atoms.

Kamma: (Sanskrit karma.) Action performed that effects future.

Metta: Selfless love and goodwill. One of the qualities of a pure mind. Metta meditation—the systemic cultivation of metta by a meditation technique.

Nadis: 72,000 subtle channels for life energy to each point in the body

Nibbana: (Sanskrit nirvana.) Extinction. Freedom from suffering; the ultimate reality; the unconditioned.

Pali: Language spoken in northern India at the time of the Buddha. Later translated into Sanskrit.

Pana: Wisdom. Cultivated by practicing Vipassana to purify the mind. The third of three trainings by which the Noble Eightfold Path is practiced. Wisdom gained by developing direct personal experience of the three characteristics of reality, beyond listening to others or intellectual analysis.

Samadhi: Concentration; control of one's mind. the second of three trainings by which the Noble Eightfold Path is practiced. When practiced by itself, it leads to states of mental absorption (jhana), but not total liberation of the mind.

Samsara: Conditioned world, world of suffering.

Sangha: Congregation; community of those who have experienced nibbana; community of Buddhist monks or nuns.

Sati: Awareness.

Satipatthana: Establishment of awareness. Eight-day study course to become established in the technique.

Shaktipat: Transmission of spiritual energy upon one person by another with a sacred word, look, or touch.

Shushumna: Central fundamental energy nadi with the ida on the left and pingala on the right.

Sila: Morality. Abstaining from physical and vocal actions that cause harm to oneself and others. The first of three trainings by which Noble Eightfold Path is practiced.

Sotapanna: First stage of enlightenment or nibbana, followed by sakadagami, anagami, and arahant.

Torus: Three-dimensional flow of energy resembling a spinning double donut, seen in 2D as the flower of life

Vipassana: Introspection, wisdom/insight that totally purifies the mind. Specifically, insight into the impermanent nature of mind and body. To know reality as it is, not as you perceive it to be.